GREAT ROOKIES
OF PRO BASKETBALL

The biographical sketches of ten basketball players who earned the National Basketball Association's coveted Rookie of the Year award. The profiles range from Westley Unseld, the NBA's most recent winner, to Don Meineke, the first man ever to win the award. Also included are Earl Monroe, Rick Barry, Jerry Lucas, Terry Dischinger, Walt Bellamy, Tom Heinsohn, Maurice Stokes and Ray Felix.

GREAT
ROOKIES
OF PRO BASKETBALL

Compiled by Zander Hollander
Illustrated with Photographs

RANDOM HOUSE · NEW YORK

CONTENTS

INTRODUCTION

They are all professional basketball players, of course, but Westley Unseld, Rick Barry, Earl Monroe, Jerry Lucas and more than a dozen other stars share something else in common.

It is a singular honor that they have won, an honor that has been bestowed upon just one gifted young man each National Basketball Association season since 1952-53. It is selection—by vote of the basketball writers in the various cities —as the official NBA "Rookie of the Year."

There is no set formula for winning the election. The rare freshman pro who scores the most points in the league has to be a strong candidate. But other factors can influence the election. For example, San Diego's outstanding Elvin Hayes, NBA scoring champion as a rookie in the 1968-69 season, wound up second in the balloting to Baltimore's Unseld, a most deserving giant, whose all-around skills appealed more to the basketball writers.

Naturally the NBA's Rookies of the Year make a distinguished lineup. Not all become superstars; one of them, Maurice Stokes, was surely on his way to that distinction when illness crippled his career. But whatever has happened since, each will always remember—and be remembered for —the very special, wonderful year when he broke into basketball's big league.

The stories of ten of these rookies are told in this book. Several other Rookies of the Year are covered in *Heroes of Pro Basketball,* another book in the Random House Pro Basketball Library.

I am grateful for the contributions of the six-man team of writers, none of them rookies, who proved they could put the ball in the basket. The lineup: Neil Amdur, *The New York Times;* Si Burick, Dayton *Daily News;* Ed Hershey, Long Island *Newsday;* Bob Rubin, *Sport* magazine; Bob Sales, Boston *Globe,* and Jack Zanger.

ZANDER HOLLANDER

GREAT ROOKIES
OF PRO BASKETBALL

1

A MOST
VALUABLE
ROOKIE

WESTLEY
UNSELD

by BOB RUBIN

Willis Reed, the New York Knicks' 6-foot 10-inch, powerful 235-pound center, had the ball at the Baltimore Bullets' foul line. He was determined to back in closer to the basket for a shot, but Baltimore's rookie center Westley Unseld, a rock of a man at 6 feet 7½ inches and 245 pounds, was just as determined that Reed would not get any closer. As the two brawny giants strained and pushed each other like angry bull elephants, the spectators in Baltimore's Civic Center that night late in the 1968-69 season could see that pro basketball is definitely a contact sport. It was the National Basketball Association's version of the irresistible force meeting the immovable object.

Though almost three inches taller than Unseld, Reed finally realized what even the league's seven-footers had learned: there was simply no way to overpower this rookie who lumbered around with tree-trunk legs and a barrel chest. So Reed was forced to shoot from the foul line. The ball fell short, bouncing off the front rim. Unseld went into action. Going high into the air, he picked off the rebound and whipped the ball out to midcourt before his feet touched the ground. There it was taken by the Bullet guard, Earl Monroe, who was off and running with fellow guard Kevin Loughery on a fast break that ended with an easy Loughery layup. As the ball dropped through the net, Unseld was still down at the other end of the court. The crowd's cheers were for Monroe and Loughery.

In the newspaper box score the next day, Unseld got credit only for a rebound on the play. But players on both teams, the real experts, knew it had been Unseld's enormous strength that had kept the very dangerous Reed out just far enough to make him miss. They knew that the key to the Bullets' fast-break layup had been Unseld's light-ning-quick pitchout. They also realized that any man who throws that kind of pitchout must be a team player, unconcerned about his own scoring. By putting the ball in motion on the fast break, he was taking himself out of the play. It all goes to prove that statistics alone can never measure a man's full value.

Although Unseld didn't score often as a rookie, he could go up for points when the occasion arose.

Indeed, the experts did not use statistics in measuring Westley Unseld's full value in the 1968-69 season. He scored just 13.8 points per game, far below the best in the league. His shooting percentages were not unusually high. Only in rebounding, where he finished second to Wilt Chamberlain with an average of 18.2 a game, did Unseld's name appear among the league leaders.

But the experts sensibly overlooked the statistics and presented Westley Unseld with the two highest honors he could receive as a first-year man. He was named Rookie of the Year. And, he was selected as the league's Most Valuable Player.

Neither honor came easily. It had been a season in which another rookie, Elvin "Big E" Hayes, led the league in scoring almost from the start of the season. He finished with more than 28 points a game.

The highest honor of all, of course, was for Unseld to be selected by his fellow players as the NBA's Most Valuable Player. The only other rookie ever to have been named MVP was Chamberlain in 1960, and even Wilt hadn't been chosen by such a wide margin. Unseld amassed 310 points to 137 for New York's Reed, the runner-up.

Being selected MVP came as a shock to Wes, who is a modest, soft-spoken man off the court. "It's very nice, but I don't know whether I deserve it or not, and I really mean that," he said. "I just don't know what to say. I'm honored that I was chosen. I'm proud to win it."

Despite his own modest opinion, Unseld clearly deserved the honor. There are only two statistics that matter to the pros—a team's win–loss record and its position in the standings. With the addition of Unseld, the Bullets went from a 36-46 record and last place in the Eastern Division to a 57-25 record and first place. He was the cohesive force that transformed the Bullets from a bunch of brilliant individuals into a team.

Unseld did the unglamorous but vital jobs— playing tough defense under the basket, grabbing rebounds, getting the ball out to the guard. By doing so, he freed his teammates for the more spectacular run-and-shoot aspects of the game. Unseld's own scoring average was of little concern to him. "I don't want to sound as if I'm bragging," he said, "but I was always taught that anybody can score 20 points a game if he shoots enough. But my coaches always asked me how many guys can make 20 rebounds a game."

Not many. But then not many players are so unselfishly dedicated to the welfare of their teams that they will concentrate almost all of their efforts on the grinding, bruising business of waging war in the backboard jungle. The Bullets were fortunate to find such a man—and they knew it.

Bob Ferry, an assistant coach who sometimes came in as Unseld's substitute at center, put it like this: "I call Wes 'the computer.' That's because as soon as you tell him something he does it. You don't have to wonder if it will happen, or if he will mess it up, or if he'll feel like doing it. No, he just does it. And he does it right every time. Things that took me ten years to learn to do, Wes can do now—because he has so much quicker re-actions than I did."

Opponents were just as awed by the Bullet rookie. Atlanta Hawk Coach Richie Guerin simply shook his head and said: "It's hard to believe that one guy could make such a difference in a team."

Westley learned to be unselfish when he was young. For one thing there were seven children in the family of Mr. and Mrs. Charles Unseld of Louisville, Kentucky. For another, Wes had parents who combined the right blend of love and discipline in raising their children. As a result, all seven went to college. Since Mr. Unseld was never wealthy, sending so many children through school called for quite an effort on his part.

"My father worked two jobs," Wes said. "He got himself a couple of heart attacks, but he made sure we got through. My father really sacrificed for us."

In return for their hard work, the Unselds expected their children to stay out of trouble. Wes learned that when he was still in grade school. "I remember my mother saying, 'If you ever get in trouble, I'll come over there and whip you in front of the whole school'," Wes said. "I never gave her the opportunity, but she'd probably do that now, too, if I messed up."

As a youngster, Wes's athletic interests were in football and baseball. He didn't care for basketball until, as an eighth-grader, he learned that his older brother George had become an established star for Louisville's Seneca High School varsity. That stirred the competitive juices within Wes. "If George could do it, so could I—or bust trying," he said.

He was no bust. Instead, he led the Seneca freshman team in scoring and rebounding. Over the summer he grew 4½ inches taller, returning to school as a 6-foot 5-inch sophomore. He made the starting varsity team at center, but was content to get the rebounds while the seniors did the shooting. As a junior the following year, his scoring average advanced only to a modest 12.1 points per game. But Kentucky sportswriters already recognized his talent on the backboards. They named him to the all-state team.

Unseld's senior year was one of the most memorable basketball seasons any Kentucky high

In basketball-mad Kentucky, Unseld and Seneca High were Number 1.

school player has ever enjoyed. The lone returning regular at Seneca High, he was burdened with more rebounding and scoring responsibilities. Wes averaged 24.5 points and 21 rebounds per game as Seneca became the first team in 30 years to repeat as state champion in Kentucky. He headed the all-state team, and was named to most of the high school All-America teams. More than 100 colleges from coast to coast showed an interest in him. After studying the offers, he decided there was no place like home. He enrolled at the University of Louisville.

Louisville was fortunate. It's hard to imagine

one player contributing more to a team than Wes did to the Cardinals. "He's got the finest mental attitude of any athlete I've ever seen in college," said John Dromo, the varsity coach when Wes was a senior. "We've never had anything like him before and won't see anything like him in the future. What makes Westley so great is his total value. He's a great player. He is without a doubt the finest young man I've met in 30 years of coaching."

As a freshman, Unseld averaged 35.8 points, making an astounding 68.6 per cent of his shots from the floor, and 23.6 rebounds a game. He led the freshman team to a 15-0 record and a preseason victory over the varsity.

As a varsity player the following season, Wes averaged 19.9 points per game, breaking the Louisville scoring record for a sophomore. He hauled down 19.4 rebounds per game to rank second in the country in that category. He was named Missouri Valley Conference "Sophomore of the Year" and was a unanimous selection to the all-conference team. He finished the storybook season by scoring 35 points and grabbing 26 rebounds against Boston College in an opening round at the National Invitation Tournament game played before some 17,000 fans at New York's Madison Square Garden. Boston College eventually won the game in triple overtime, eliminating Louis-

ville. But Unseld was still selected to the All-NIT team.

Wes's junior year was virtually a repeat of his sophomore season—except that more people began to notice him. He averaged 18.8 points and 19.4 rebounds per game (third best in the country), nearly identical statistics to the ones he had compiled as a sophomore. This year, however, he not only made the All-MVC team, but several of the All-America teams.

As a senior, he made every All-America team on the strength of a 23-point and 18.3-rebound average. In three seasons on the varsity, Unseld led Louisville teams to a combined 64-19 record.

The pros were understandably impressed. The Kentucky Colonels of the new American Basketball Association, who used Louisville as their base, offered Unseld the chance to continue to play in his hometown. Their three-year, $500,-000 contract made the offer tempting. But the Colonels made the mistake of publicizing their offer by running it as a full-page advertisement in the Louisville newspapers. The sensitive Unseld didn't like this. "I didn't appreciate them making it public," he said. "I didn't want everybody to

The University of Louisville never had a better all-around player than hometown boy Wes Unseld (31).

know what I was getting. I figured that was my own business."

For that and other reasons, Wes signed to play in Baltimore, even though the Bullets were offering him only a little more than half of what the Colonels had promised. "Money was important, but I had my degree and I figured I could always make a living," he explained. "You never miss money if you've never had it, so I didn't lose any sleep over it. Besides, when you play basketball, you want to know how you'll do against the Russells and the Chamberlains. You never know how good you are until you play against the best. You have to find out for yourself."

It didn't take long for Wes and everyone else to find out that he belonged in the NBA. After he signed with the Bullets in June, 1968, he immediately moved to Baltimore and began to work out three times a week with the other Bullets who were living in town during the off-season.

"He can play," was the simple way that Kevin Loughery summed up his first impression of Wes in those workouts. "He's so strong—and so quick. He gets the ball out on the break and he moves much better with the ball than I thought he

In one of his rookie games against Milwaukee, Unseld displayed his natural talents as a leader when he restrained teammate Earl Monroe, angered by a referee's decision.

would. When he goes to the basket, he gets there. It's that simple. He's almost impossible to stop because he's so strong he doesn't lose control of the ball."

Before long, he changed a lot of opinions. And he proved that a basketball player doesn't have to shoot all the time to be the best player on the court. Or, for that matter, to become the Most Valuable Player in basketball's toughest league.

2
THE DROPOUT
DROPS IN

DON
MEINEKE

by SI BURICK

Donald Edward "Monk" Meineke was an angry and frustrated young lad. As a freshman at
Chaminade High School in Dayton, Ohio, he had
been cut from the basketball squad on the first
day of practice. The following year, although he
already stood 6-feet 1-inch tall, he was not even
invited to try out for the varsity. Soon he lost all
interest in his schoolbooks, and started to fail
most of his courses.

"This school stuff is for the birds," he told himself, and he dropped out of Chaminade at the
age of sixteen.

He took a job at the Inland Manufacturing
Company, one of several General Motors plants
in Dayton. The job was strictly for the unskilled.
His assignment night after night was to remove

19

excess pieces of rubber from shock absorbers. Anyone could have done it.

Then one hot, late August night, Don paused in his labors and asked himself why he could not get something better than this repetitious, monotonous job. When the foreman saw Meineke daydreaming, he growled, "What are you standing around for, Slim? There's work to be done."

Gathering up his courage, Meineke asked for a promotion. The foreman, who was scarcely 5 feet tall, grinned and replied: "What else do you know, Slim?"

Don Meineke got the message. He wasn't qualified for anything but common labor. When he signed out that morning, he knew he would never be back. School was about to reopen, and now he understood that there was no future for a fellow who did not have at least a high school education. The little foreman was right. *What else did he know?*

Meineke had no trouble convincing his father and stepmother that he should return to school, but he knew that Chaminade, a parochial school, was not for him. He would enroll instead at Wilbur Wright, the neighborhood public high school named for the native Dayton inventor.

Wright High accepted him with the provision that he would have to take his complete sophomore year over again. Could he try out for the basketball team? Yes—but as a transfer student. He would have to sit out one year. That would leave only one year of eligibility since his senior year would actually be his fifth in high school.

Like most kids in the neighborhood, Don had started playing basketball in the backyards and alleys. Somebody had nailed a peachbasket to a utility pole. Someone else had a battered old basketball. Don, as a seventh-grader, stood only 5-feet 2-inches tall. The other kids quickly gave him his nickname. Meineke was slurred so it sounded like "Monkey," and that became "Monk" for short.

By the eighth grade, the kids learned about the Boys' Club, where there were regular basketball hoops and backboards and a court to play on. But the Boys' Club was 4 miles away. If Don and his friends were unsuccessful in "hitching" a ride, they would walk to the club and home again. That proved how eager they were to play basketball.

One day at the club, Meineke met Chuck Grigsby, a youngster his own age, who attended Stivers High. Grigsby would become Meineke's occasional teammate, occasional rival, and lifetime pal. Without him, Don never would have gotten to college.

The Boys' Club was perfect for Meineke's need. Even though he was frustrated in his basketball ambitions at Chaminade, he began to learn to play the game at the club. And during the year he was an ineligible sophomore at Wilbur Wright, he and Chuck Grigsby played on the same independent team at the club. Their team not only won a city championship, but also went undefeated.

As a junior, Meineke spurted up to 6-feet 5-inches. Dwight Bushong, the coach at Wilbur Wright, invited him to try out for center on the varsity. Don did, but there were new problems. High school basketball was more disciplined than it had been on the independent team. He had never learned much about team play. He was often guilty of fumbling. And, at 155 pounds, he lacked stamina. That year Wright lost the city championship to Stivers High. The star for the winning team in the title game was Chuck Grigsby.

Though his basketball eligibility came to an end at the beginning of his senior year, Don was determined to get his diploma. To remain active, he joined the Millette Confectionary amateur club, while completing his senior year studies. One of his Millette teammates was Grigsby, who had graduated from Stivers but had decided to work for a year before trying college.

One night during a city amateur tournament, Tom Blackburn, then the basketball coach at the

University of Dayton, visited the Millette dressing room. Meineke and Grigsby were getting
dressed at adjoining lockers. Blackburn, address-
ing Grigsby, talked of the Dayton Flyers' ambi-
tion to become a major basketball power. He offered Grigsby a scholarship. Then Blackburn
turned to Don and suggested a basketball scholarship for him, too.

At first, Meineke believed that the coach had
extended the offer to him only because he didn't
want to seem to slight him. But Blackburn called
Meineke several times. When Grigsby accepted
Dayton's bid, Meineke was still filled with
doubts. He was worried that both the competition
and the books would prove too tough. But finally
Don decided that he, too, would accept the grant-
in-aid.

The Dayton freshmen played a regular college
schedule, and on Sundays they also performed
in a local Amateur Athletic Union league, wear-
ing the uniforms of the Zimmerman Construction
Company. Meineke and Grigsby helped the construction firm win the district and state AAU ti-
tles, then reach the National AAU quarter-finals.
The competition was just what Meineke needed.
For once he had reason to have confidence in himself. He had grown to his full height (6 feet 7½
inches) and his body filled out to 200 pounds.

The freshman year was followed by three won-

derful years on the varsity. Both Meineke and his friend Grigsby earned starting berths as sophomores—Don at center and Chuck at forward.

As juniors, they led the Flyers into the finals of the National Invitational Tournament in New York City, where they lost to Brigham Young University. They took Dayton into the NIT finals again as seniors, before losing the title to LaSalle. In three years, the Flyers won 79 games and lost only 18.

But Meineke's biggest thrill as a collegian occurred in his senior year, just before the NIT playoff, when he played his final game on the Dayton home court. He already had won mention on some All-America teams. He had established twenty team records at the school. And any doubts he had once felt about academic matters now must have seemed remote. His grades had zoomed to the B-plus level.

In that final home game—against Miami of Ohio—where Coach Blackburn took Meineke out with a few minutes left on the clock, the sellout crowd of 5,800 rose and applauded for several minutes. So did Meineke's own teammates on the bench. The referees, having no choice, held up the game for several minutes. "It was a haunting

Meineke, shown tipping in a shot against New York University, put the University of Dayton on the basketball map.

thunder of sound," wrote one Dayton sportswriter, who reported that he had never heard
such an ovation before.

Professional scouts had been watching Dayton
for three years. Now the Fort Wayne Zollner Pistons (later to become the Detroit Pistons) made
Meineke their first choice in the National Basketball Association's annual draft. Another impossible dream had come true. But first Meineke had
to meet another stern test. At Fort Wayne, Coach
Paul Birch advised his rookie he would have to
play forward. The Pistons already had two expe-
rienced centers who were taller than Meineke—
6-foot-9 Larry Foust and 6-foot-11 Charlie Share.
But Birch also emphasized the fact that he had
room for a younger starter. Don had a chance to
beat out either Fred Schaus or Jack Kerris at forward.

The adjustment to forward was doubly hard.
As a college center, Meineke had always played
with his back to his own basket. As a pro forward,
he would have to face the goal. As a center, he
had relied on hook shots and setting up teammates with a pass off. He had no set shot; he had
no jump shot. He would need to develop both.

*Meineke was given a free ride by his Dayton teammates
as a reward for his 37-point night against Arizona in the
NIT.*

Furthermore, in college, he scarcely ever had to dribble the ball. Now he must learn to do this, too. And then there was the new emphasis on defense. At Dayton, he usually had guarded the opposing center, whose back was also to the basket. Now he would guard a forward, facing the goal.

There was only one thing to do—work, work, work. Meineke was willing. Shortly before the 1952-53 championship season began, he wrested away Jack Kerris' starting role at forward. And in pre-season exhibition games against the Minneapolis Lakers and the New York Knicks, Meineke earned Most Valuable Player honors. It was a start toward greater things.

Meineke gradually improved his dribbling and shooting. He worked out a way to receive passes closer to the basket, which made shooting those new sets and jumps easier. He also learned that the NBA was no league in which to take your time. If you delayed your shot, it was sure to be blocked.

While he was learning, he came up against some harsh experiences. One occurred before a packed audience in Fort Wayne. The Pistons were facing Minneapolis. The Lakers' center, George Mikan, was considered the finest player in the game at the time. But Meineke had made it his business to study the giant's mannerisms.

He observed that almost every time Mikan went up for a rebound, he took the ball over his left shoulder.

The first time George went up for a rebound, Don shifted defensive assignments with center Larry Foust, then calmly reached up and stole the ball away.

It was a bold thing to do against the NBA's top star. But the big crowd's approval encouraged Meineke to try the same trick again. As Meineke leaped for a second steal, Mikan let his elbow fly. It caught the rookie flush on the mouth. *Crunch!* Reeling with pain, Meineke called time. And when the Fort Wayne trainer helped him unlock his bleeding mouth, Don's upper dental plate— the result of a college collision—fell out in little pieces. It was as embarrassing as it was painful.

Later, when he was back in the game, Monk lined up beside Mikan on a free throw.

"You all right, kid?" Mikan asked.

"Yeah, I'm okay."

"Did I do that to your mouth?"

"Yes, you did."

"Well, I'm awfully sorry," the big man from Minneapolis grunted, and then went on about his business.

More embarrassment was to come. Meineke had a post-game date with a pretty bank employee he had met when he deposited his $3,000

Fort Wayne bonus check. (His first-year salary was only $6,500.) On a previous date, the girl had complimented Don on his "pretty teeth." He couldn't bring himself to admit they were the "store-bought" variety. Lacking a spare plate, he met her with bowed head.

"Don't worry," the girl said. "You still look nice without any teeth." Don's confidence was restored immediately. His teeth were restored soon after.

The Pistons, playing a "pick-and-screen" type of offense, were having a good year. But the trend in the NBA was toward the fast break. This worried the rookie from Dayton, who had never played the run-and-shoot game. The Pistons, too, were departing from their old methodical patterns. The swing in the NBA was more and more toward jump shooters. Meineke just wasn't one of them.

Meineke was learning, as every rookie has to, that the season is a long one. Travel in the wintertime was often difficult. Too many meals had to be consumed on the run. The life of a pro had its moments of fun, too, but where did his future really lie?

Don was gaining confidence in his ability to compete against the world's greatest basketball players. But thinking of the years ahead, he decided on a personal five-year plan. He had ob-

served that five years was about the average for
NBA careers. His future, he decided, belonged
in sales, not basketball. He hoped to test his ability as a salesman during the off-season.

But Meineke's long-range plans did not affect
his play as a rookie. In 68 games he averaged
10.7 points. Although that kind of scoring pace
is not eye-catching by today's standards, in the
1952-53 season only three NBA players averaged
more than 20 points a game. In addition, Meineke
pulled down 466 rebounds. After helping get
Fort Wayne into the playoffs, Don was a natural
choice as the NBA's first official "Rookie of the
Year."

The following summer, he sold heating and air-
conditioning units for a Dayton firm, and discovered he had made another good decision. He
loved selling.

His five-year plan was moving on schedule.
Big leapers like Mel Hutchins and George Yard-
ley came to the Pistons. Meineke became a defensive specialist, and teammates referred to him
as "The Stopper." After four years, Fort Wayne
traded him to the Cincinnati Royals. And when
that season ended, in 1957, the selling field
seemed more appealing than basketball. Living
up to his plan, he announced his retirement from
the game.

Having proved that he could be a success in

sports, the one-time dropout wanted to show that he could achieve success in a field where he could utilize his knowledge, too. Today, after several steps up in the business world, he is a successful sales manager for WLW-D, a Dayton television station.

3
HE
TRIED
HARDER

RAY
FELIX

by BOB RUBIN

When Ray Felix was a sixth-grader in New York's Harlem, he already stood 6-feet 1-inch tall. He can vividly remember the day the teacher measured him in front of the whole class because she was curious about his exact height. He also recalls how the rest of the class giggled at him while he stood against the wall. He was embarrassed, ashamed and hurt when he heard them. "The other kids always made fun of me because I was so much bigger than anyone else," Felix said. "I was never part of the group. I always had to go out on my own looking for friends."

Youngsters who are different from the crowd are always targets for teasing. Usually no one means harm, but often the taunts can do damage to a sensitive boy or girl. Ray Felix, who was to grow to be 6-feet 11-inches tall by age 18, could easily have become shy and withdrawn as so many tall youngsters do. His shoulders might have become permanently rounded and his spine bent in an effort to slouch down and look smaller. But Felix did none of these things. He learned to live with his "problem." Proudly, he stood tall, ignored the taunts, and took up basketball, one of the few activities where it is an advantage to be bigger than everyone else.

But basketball didn't come easily. Ray was one of the first skyscraping centers. In his day, the 7-footers weren't expected to have the speed and the moves and the agility of the Wilt Chamberlains and Nate Thurmonds and Lew Alcindors who followed them. The giants were something new to coaches, so these big players had to be developed from scratch.

Ray posed an additional problem. At the outset he showed little natural talent. His coordination, reflexes and jumping ability were not outstanding, and he was downright slow. He was also clumsy with his hands, which made it difficult for him to catch and hold onto a ball. At his peak he weighed only 217 pounds, which made him far too thin for his height. More muscular men could shove him around by using sheer strength.

But as great as these handicaps were, Felix had two tremendous assets working for him. One, of

Everyone seemed awed by Felix's height.

course, was his great height. The other—and by
far the more important of the two—was his un-
quenchable determination.

"We had to make him into a ballplayer," said
Clair Bee, who coached Ray in 1950 at Long Island University and later as a rookie for the Baltimore Bullets of the National Basketball Association. "You could just tell from looking at him

that he wasn't a 'natural.' Whatever he accomplished in basketball, he accomplished through sheer effort. He never quit trying."

Without Felix's big effort, the 1953-54 Bullet season might have been a complete blank. The skinny rookie center brought an enthusiasm to the court that carried over to his teammates on several occasions. Even so, the Baltimore five finished last in the league's Eastern Division, winning only 16 games and losing 56. They lost all 21 of their road games and 16 of the 20 contests they played at neutral sites. "Without Felix," Bee recalled with a shudder, "we wouldn't have had to bother to show up."

When the season was over, Ray's name was at the top of every Bullet statistical column, except assists. He grabbed 958 rebounds, made 41.7 per cent of his shots, and had an average of 17.6 points per game. In all three of those categories he ranked among the top five leaders in the NBA. By today's standards, a 17.6 average wouldn't sound so impressive. But pro basketball has changed drastically. Instead of scoring upwards of 100 points per game the way today's teams do, the teams of 1953-54 averaged about 70 to 85 points. Thus individual averages were relatively lower. It wasn't until the following season, 1954-55, that the 24-second rule went into effect and radically changed the game into a faster, high-scoring sport. The new rule prevented stalling by forcing a team to shoot within 24 seconds after gaining possession of the ball.

In his rookie season, Ray's two best individual efforts were made against two of the best teams. He scored 32 points against the Eastern Division champions, the New York Knickerbockers, who had 6-foot 8-inch veteran Connie Simmons in the pivot. Then he repeated the 32-point total in a game against the world champion Minneapolis Lakers. That was an even greater feat, for the Lakers were sparked by George Mikan, a 240-pound, 6-foot 10-inch center who was considered the best player, big or small, in the game.

Felix got around the giants by making effective use of his height and his long arm-span. Using either his left or right hand, he let go with untouchable hook shots. He would also follow up on his teammates' shots, which occasionally rewarded him with a rebound and an easy layup. On defense, he kept his huge hands in the air, making opponents think twice about trying to drive in his vicinity. When a shot went up, he was consistently in the proper position for the rebound.

Equally important, Felix was a team player. Though he led all scorers in both games, he never stopped searching out his teammates to see if they had a better shot. Unfortunately, his team-

Ray made use of his long reach to tie up Detroit's Walt Dukes.

mates didn't do the same. "Ray's doing an even better job for us than often appears because I'm afraid our other men haven't helped him much at working the ball in," Bee told a reporter at the time. "Ray is such a sincere, conscientious boy, he makes coaching a pleasure. I've got a lot of worries trying to get this club on the right foot, but Felix isn't one of them."

A highlight of Ray's rookie season came in the 1954 All-Star game when he was chosen the starting Eastern Division center and once again had to battle the great Mikan. "I was nervous," Ray said. "Here I was, just a rookie, playing my first All-Star game against a man everyone thought was the greatest center who ever lived. I had to wonder if I could do the job."

Ray did the job far better than anyone had expected. "Ray played Mikan hard," Bee noted. "Mikan had those terrifically sharp elbows and would use them on anyone who came too close. But Ray hung in there. He refused to be destroyed, and in those days Mikan was destroying just about everyone in the league." Mikan scored 18 points but so did Felix. And Ray also held his own in the always vital battle for rebounds. The East won, 98-93, and after the game all the players agreed that the result would have been different without Felix.

Felix was so impressive that he was chosen as the NBA's Rookie of the Year.

When Ray was born in Harlem on December 10, 1930, there was no reason to think he would eventually be exceptionally tall. His mother and five sisters were above average in height, but not unusually so. His father, who died when Ray was five, was not quite 6 feet tall. But when young Ray began to gulp down enough food for two meals at a single sitting, the Felix family began to suspect that there might be something special about him.

It wasn't until Ray reached high school, however, that he began to utilize his height in sports. Until then, his favorite game had been softball. But the Metropolitan High basketball coach and players noticed him (he was hard to miss), and talked him into trying out. It proved a blessing for both Ray and the team. Basketball gave him a purpose and a goal, something to strive for.

There were problems at first. "I was awkward and clumsy and I didn't even have a pair of sneakers," Felix said. "It's not like today when the boys start playing very young and learn the game when they're still youngsters. I started very late, especially for a big boy, and I really didn't know what I was doing for quite a while. But I loved the game, and from then on I began to 'eat basketball' for breakfast, lunch and dinner. I'd even dream about the game at night."

Ray played anywhere and everywhere he could. He got into countless games at "the Oval," a popular meeting ground for ambitious young ballplayers near City College. He traveled out of Manhattan to Sunnyside Gardens and the Rockaways in Queens County. He went to Brooklyn to play in a Young Men's Hebrew Association league, although he was not Jewish. "Anywhere there was a league, I played," he recalled.

Gradually, painfully, Felix began to get better. By the time he was a senior at Metropolitan High, he made the All-City team. Considering the tremendous caliber of basketball players in New York, it was an honor indeed. But Ray was seldom challenged seriously in high school, simply because there were so few opponents anywhere near as tall. Ray was still awkward and still made mistakes. But he could get away with them.

Not until he got to Long Island University and came under the guidance of Bee and his assistant coach, "Pic" Picariello, did he really begin to learn what hard work was.

Bee turned Felix over to Picariello, who stood 5-foot-6. Though they looked like Mutt and Jeff, Felix and his little teacher got along very well.

"If ever there was a 'made' ballplayer, it was Ray," said Picariello. "All he had going for himself was heart. Work, work, work—that's how he did it, that's how he made himself into one heck of a player. He had what I call the five D's of basketball: discipline, desire, determination, dedication and drive. His story should be a terrific incentive to anyone who doesn't have the greatest talent in the world but who really wants to make it."

Under Picariello's guidance, Ray did pushups and squat thrusts, shadow-boxed, skipped rope, ran laps backward and forward and went through seemingly endless varieties of jumping and agility drills. Bee and Picariello painted footsteps on the gym floor and made Felix walk his way through them so he would learn the proper moves of a center. They strapped blocks to his hands with rubber bands to make sure he learned to catch the ball with his fingertips. Through it all, Ray never complained. "I figured it was for my own betterment," said Felix philosophically.

Because of his hard work, Ray averaged 22 points per game for the LIU freshmen in 1950. The team was counting on his being the starting center for the powerful varsity the following year. But before the season began, police discovered that many LIU players had been participants in a nationwide scandal. The players had accepted bribes from gamblers to "shave" points. That is, they had tried to keep their winning margin within a certain number of points so that the gamblers would win their bets. One of the few good LIU players not involved in the scandal was Ray Felix. "I was shocked, very shocked," he said. "I knew all the guys, I considered them my friends. They made a terrible mistake."

As a result of the scandal, the guilty players were suspended from school. LIU was pressured to drop basketball. But Felix finished college, playing semi-pro basketball, then professional ball for a team in the now-extinct American Basketball League. He was the ABL's leading scorer and starred in the league's championship playoffs. But he was just biding his time until he grad-

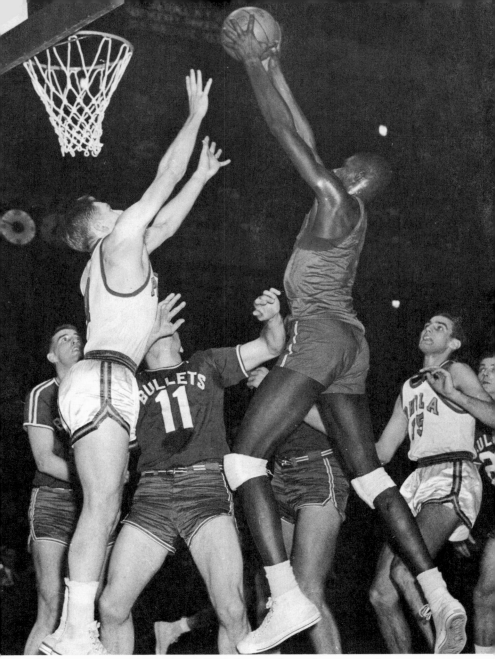

Thin but strong, Felix pulled down rebounds vigorously.

uated. When he did, he turned down an offer to play for the Harlem Globetrotters because he wanted to sign with the NBA's Bullets and be re-united with Coach Bee. "I felt I owed quite a bit to Mr. Bee," he explained. "He was good to me. Basketball was good to me."

And big Ray was good to basketball.

After his sensational rookie season, Felix was sold to the New York Knicks. The faltering Bullets were virtually bankrupt and selling players was the only way they could raise money. (It didn't help; they went out of business before the start of the 1954-55 season. Baltimore did get another franchise years later, which was and still is called the Bullets.)

Ray played more than five full seasons with the Knicks before being traded to Minneapolis during the 1959-60 season. The following year, the Lakers moved to Los Angeles and Felix ended his career there in 1962. For a nine-year professional career his scoring average was 10.9 points per game.

Today Ray Felix tries to help youngsters the way he was helped. He is the director of the Edenwald Community Center in Harlem. "I try to teach kids never to become discouraged," he says. "I tell them that if they just keep trying things will turn out all right. I tell them it happened to me."

4

MAURICE
THE
MAGNIFICENT

MAURICE STOKES

by NEIL AMDUR

Maurice Stokes moved down the court with his strong and graceful stride. He took a lead pass from Rochester teammate Bobby Wanzer and saw a small opening as he drove through the middle. The opening lasted no more than an instant, however, for two New York Knickerbockers converged on Stokes, catching him between them. As Stokes went up toward the basket, there was a collision of bodies. Maurice hung in the air momentarily, then fell to the wooden floor under the basket as the crowd roared.

Immediately he looked up and saw that the white nets attached to the rim were still swaying —a sign that his shot had been good. A smile spread across Stokes' broad face. A teammate helped him to his feet and Maurice moved down

49

the court, the roar of the crowd still echoing in his ears. Stokes had survived his first grueling test in professional basketball.

The scene was Madison Square Garden, in the opening game of the 1955-56 season, and the historic New York arena was jammed to capacity. The crowd had come not only to root for the hometown Knicks, but to inspect Maurice Stokes, the highly regarded 6-foot 7-inch rookie who was playing for the Rochester Royals.

Less than a year earlier, Stokes had been a hero during another visit to New York City. As a senior at tiny St. Francis College in Loretto, Pennsylvania, he had been a unanimous choice for the Most Valuable Player award in the National Invitation Tournament.

Impressive as his performance in the NIT had been, Stokes' professional debut against the Knicks was even more spectacular. He made 11 field goals and 10 of 11 foul shots for 32 points. He also pulled down 20 rebounds and had the New York writers talking about the birth of a new pro superstar.

Maurice continued to distinguish himself in his second professional game. Against Syracuse, he scored 17 points, grabbed 20 rebounds and personally took command of the game. When he was not driving to the basket for twisting layups, Stokes was blocking out Syracuse players with

the finesse of a player who had been in the NBA
for years.

The Philadelphia Warriors were the next team
to face the Stokes magic. One of the physically
strongest teams in the NBA, the Warriors had the
idea that they could intimidate Maurice with
some rough treatment under the backboards.

"Stokes has to be taught a lesson—and quick,"
one of the Warrior veterans said before the game.

But it was Stokes who taught the lesson. The
rookie collected 26 points and 20 rebounds and
had Neil Johnston, the Philadelphia center and
one of the game's great scorers, shaking his
head. In his first three games as a professional,
Stokes had totaled 75 points, 60 rebounds and 19
assists. It was one of the most impressive NBA
debuts of the 1950s.

But his start was not all glory. In the opening
game against the Knickerbockers, he received a
kick in the head that left him face-down on the
floor. In another early-season game, this time
against the Boston Celtics, he learned the rules
under which he would have to live as a professional. A big, tough Celtic forward, known
around the league as a "hatchet man," faked a
stumble early in the game and invited Stokes to
drive around him. Maurice, ever the opportunist,
lunged at the chance, but as he drove he was
jolted by the Celtic's body block.

When the Boston player returned to his bench, he was smiling, but not at his own dirty deed. "Stokes hits back, too," the player told his teammates as he pointed to the welt on his side where Stokes' big shoulders had dug into him.

Red Auerbach, the fiery coach of the Celtics, quickly became a Stokes supporter. "Stokes is no 'rookie'," Auerbach said between bites of his familiar cigar. "He was ready for this league when he was in college. Nothing will stop him."

"There's nothing more I have to know about this fellow," said another coach after Maurice had scored 21 points, grabbed 19 rebounds and intimidated the opposition's top scorer on defense. "He's good and he's ready. Why knock ourselves out trying to make him timid? He won't be backed down. If I keep trying to disprove this, I'll end up with a player of mine hurt."

Most players in their first season of pro basketball spend much of their time sitting on the bench, watching the veterans and listening to the coach. They are fortunate if the veterans will even speak to them. This is known as the "silent treatment" and continues until the rookie has proven himself.

Stokes was the exception. The Royals refused to treat Maurice like a rookie, though actually they had no choice. He was simply too good, too strong, too dominant a player to sit on the bench.

He had to learn by slugging it out under the boards with the best players in the game.

At 6 feet 7 inches, Maurice was not quite tall enough to play against the gigantic NBA centers. So he had to become quick enough and smart enough to stop the league's top forwards—men like Paul Arizin, Dolph Schayes and Bob Pettit. As the season progressed, praise for Stokes began to build. Soon such nicknames as "Maurice The Magnificent," "Mighty Mo," and "The Stoker" appeared regularly in the sports pages.

At the halfway point of the season someone asked Al Cervi, the Syracuse coach, who he thought was the best rookie. "The answer to that has to be Stokes," he said. "But it could go further. He may very well be the best player in the league!"

On the court Maurice looked like a bull as he wedged his wide, thickly-muscled frame in front of bigger men for rebounds, position and points. "He's almost impossible to move out from underneath the basket," said one opponent. "It would take a tank to do it."

Off the court, Maurice had the look of a college professor. He wore horn-rimmed glasses and conservative Ivy League sports jackets and slacks. As rugged and powerful as Stokes appeared during the game, he had a controlled, intellectual air when he was away from the violence.

His quiet, sensitive personality was the product of a closely knit family and home life. He was born in 1933 in Pittsburgh, Pennsylvania, where his father worked in the steel mills. Maurice learned his basketball in the rugged playgrounds of the city, where an elbow was legal as long as it didn't get you into a fight you couldn't win. Once a playground opponent accidentally stuck a finger into Stokes' eye. Surgeons had to remove a piece of the eye and Maurice had to wear a patch and dark glasses for a long time. But the injury never hindered his shooting, nor his determination to succeed in a game that demanded constant practice.

He attended Westinghouse High School in Pittsburgh, a local basketball power. But Maurice was overshadowed by teammate Ed Fleming, who would later become his pro teammate. Stokes was not selected for any of the high school all-star teams; in fact, one college coach described him as "too big and too slow." Even so, ten schools thought enough of Stokes' size and potential to offer him a basketball scholarship. Maurice decided against the larger schools and settled on tiny St. Francis College, where he could play regularly and be close to home.

In the third game of his college career, as a freshman playing for the varsity, he scored 32 points and grabbed 28 rebounds against Villanova before fouling out. St. Francis lost, 94-86, but after the game Al Severance, the Villanova coach, said, "Stokes is the greatest freshman I've ever seen."

But Loretto, Pennsylvania, was a long way from the big time, and national recognition comes hard for players from small schools. Stokes spent most of his college career as a strictly local hero. Not until his senior year did Maurice receive the general acclaim that would carry him to the pro ranks with an impressive set of credentials.

The acclaim came in the National Invitation Tournament when Stokes led St. Francis into the semi-finals against nationally-ranked Dayton. Scarcely anybody gave St. Francis a chance. But Stokes was magnificent. A New York sportswriter called his performance "the greatest one-man show in the history of the NIT."

Stokes seemed to be everywhere during the game. He scored his team's first nine points and then continued to throw in jump shots, hook shots and set shots. St. Francis lost, 79-73, but Stokes finished the game with 43 points and 19 rebounds.

His performance prompted Joe Lapchick, then the coach of the New York Knickerbockers, to recall other great moments he had witnessed on the court. "Stokes was better as an all-around bas-ketball player than George Mikan was the night he scored 53 against Rhode Island State," Lap-chick said. "All Mikan did was hook in the points. Stokes did everything a player could do with a basketball."

Following the tournament, Stokes turned down lucrative offers from the Harlem Globetrotters and an industrial league team. "I want to play with the best," he said. He was referring to the NBA.

"The pros are bigger and stronger than college players," said Stokes, midway through his first season at Rochester, "and you're always working against fellows 6-9 and 6-10. But rebounding isn't enough. What you have to learn is not to wait. If you wait, you're shut out."

What made Stokes so formidable was his fear-less work under the basket. Rochester had good guards who could dribble and shoot from the outside. If they missed the shot, there was Stokes, pushing and shoving for the important offen-sive rebound.

Once, against the Knickerbockers, Stokes was waging his customary battle under the basket.

"Cut that out," a Knick player said to Stokes as the two exchanged elbows and hips.

"If you can't take it, move out," Stokes an-swered as he gave the New Yorker another

Stokes (12) powered through opponents to tip in shots.

healthy shove, extended his arms and took down another rebound.

It was this dedication and drive, an unquench-able will to succeed, that brought Stokes 1,125 points in the 1955-56 season for a 16.8 average. And it was his unselfish team play that gave him 328 assists, third-best in the league. He was the only frontcourt player among the NBA's nine as-sist leaders. It was the same kind of performance that earned him the league's Rookie of the Year award.

The following season, proving that he was no one-year flash, Stokes scored 1,124 points (15.6 average) and set a league rebounding record with 1,256, an average of 17.4 a game.

But a year later, after the Royals moved to Cin-cinnati, a freak injury presented Maurice with the biggest challenge of his life. And it brought his pro career to a tragic and untimely end.

His trouble began on March 12, 1958, in a game against the Minneapolis Lakers. In typical Stokes fashion, he had leaped above a pack of players for a rebound. But he was knocked off balance and fell to the floor, slamming his head against the court. Revived with smelling salts, Maurice returned to action and finished the game with 24 points. But the blow to his head had done its damage.

Three days later, still in pain, Stokes played 39

minutes in the final game of a playoff series against the Detroit Pistons. He scored 12 points and grabbed 15 rebounds. But during the plane ride back to Cincinnati, Stokes lost consciousness. Doctors diagnosed his illness as a form of sleeping sickness, brought on by the head injury. The disease left him completely paralyzed and helpless in a hospital.

Stokes' most courageous performance took place not on the basketball court but in a hospital bed and in a wheelchair. Basketball fans every-

Despite his tragic illness, Maurice was in good spirits when he visited pro stars Tom Heinsohn, Bob Cousy, Jack Twyman, Oscar Robertson and Bill Russell.

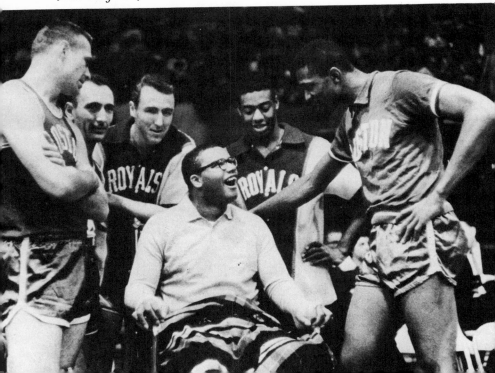

where, and many people who had never seen a game, focused on Maurice as he fought his way back from unconsciousness and attempted to regain at least partial use of his body. His magnificent 240-pound physique, once the terror of the NBA, shrunk to 160 pounds before he was able to begin a program of daily physical therapy.

Jack Twyman, Maurice's teammate on the Royals, became the stricken star's legal guardian and assumed responsibility for raising the money to pay his heavy medical expenses. Every summer the NBA's top players donate their services in an annual all-star game to raise money for Stokes' continuing rehabilitation program.

Maurice has never fully recovered, and still remains confined to a hospital. Nevertheless, in many small ways his progress has been remarkable.

And for those who had the good fortune to see Maurice The Magnificent in all his glory, none of the tragedy of his later life could ever dim their memories of this great player and outstanding individual.

"There's no telling how great a career Maurice would have had," Red Auerbach said. As it was, in three seasons Stokes had averaged 16.4 points a game and brought a new dimension to the league with his aggressive, unselfish play.

5
THE
TOMMY
GUNNER

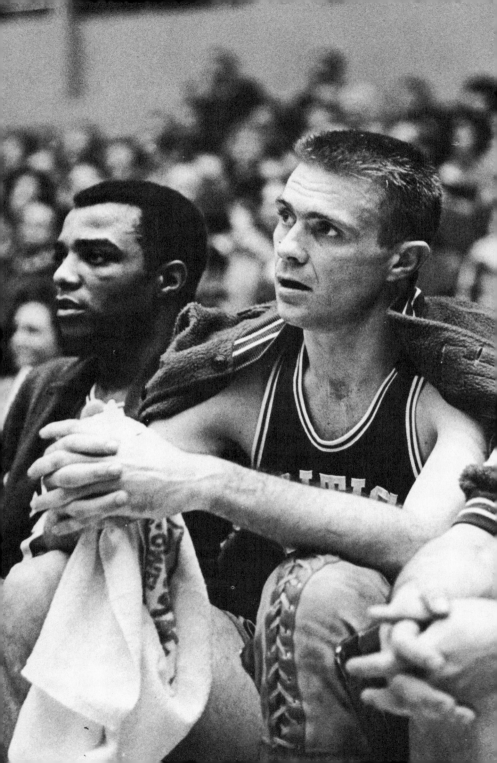

TOM
HEINSOHN

by BOB SALES

Rickety old Boston Garden was bedlam. The fans stood in the aisles whistling and shrieking and clapping their hands for Tommy Heinsohn. Although the Bostic Celtic forward had fouled out of the game, he had given his fans something to cheer about—37 points and 23 rebounds —in the final game of his sparkling rookie season.

But if Heinsohn did not seem to react joyously to the kind hometown crowd he had his reasons. For the game between the Celtics and the St. Louis Hawks was still in progress. They were playing the seventh and final game of the National Basketball Association playoffs of the 1956-57 season. The stakes were high: the winner would be the world champion of professional basketball.

Head bowed, his shoulders drooping, Heinsohn walked slowly to the Celtic bench. He slumped into a seat and pulled a towel over his crew cut, shutting out the action on the floor and hiding the tears in his eyes. He could not watch the rest of the game.

The Celtics had been leading, 121-119, with three minutes left in the second overtime when Heinsohn fouled out. Heinsohn had scored 8 of his 37 points in that overtime period. Those three minutes seemed to last forever.

Heinsohn did not see the Hawks tie the score with two-and-a-half minutes to go. He did not see Frank Ramsey's free throw put the Celtics in front. He did not see Bill Russell block Med Park's shot or Ramsey hit a 20-footer that put the Celtics in front by three points. He didn't see Park and the Celtics' Jim Loscutoff exchange free throws.

But he did peek out from under the towel when St. Louis player-coach Alex Hannum whipped a pass the length of the court with a mere second left. The ball rebounded off the backboard into the hands of St. Louis' Bob Pettit, who flipped up a shot that rolled off the front rim. No good! The Celtics were winners, 125-123. The Celtics were now world champions.

Heinsohn leaped into the air, both fists over his head. Celtic Coach Red Auerbach, a program rolled tightly in his left hand, hugged him. The crowd poured onto the court. Everybody wanted to pat Tommy Heinsohn on the back. It was a great way to end a grand season.

A couple of old pros, Bob Cousy and Bill Sharman, really appreciated what Heinsohn had done for their Boston team. Both had played seven seasons in the NBA, and each of them had dreamed of the day his team would win the championship. The final victory over St. Louis had been a trying experience for both. Cousy, who had averaged 20.6 points a game during the season, hit on only two of 20 shots from the field against the Hawks. Sharman, the team scoring

Rookie Heinsohn and Coach Auerbach jumped for joy as the Celtics won the first of their many NBA championships.

leader with a 21.1 average during the regular season, was just slightly better. He hit three of 20.

But the raw-boned rookie from Holy Cross College had scored on more than half of the field-goal shots he tried.

"The kid is the greatest," Cousy repeated again and again to anyone who would listen in the locker room after the game. "What pressure! And how he played under it!"

Sharman agreed. "I never saw such a game played by a man under such pressure," he said, shaking his head in disbelief. "Heinie—a great game and a great ballplayer."

Heinsohn had been aware of the pressure on him. He also knew that Cousy and Sharman were tight, that they couldn't find the basket with their shots. He knew that someone had to carry the load. He did the job himself.

"Sure I felt the pressure," he said. "Anyone would. But if the shot's there, take it. I took 'em."

The shot was there 33 times; that is, if you count the shots that Heinsohn *made* be there. Often he would drive in, dribbling with one hand and using the other for a battering-ram to hold off the opponent. Other times the shot was one of Heinsohn's flat line drives which he shot from the baseline and around the key. Other times he muscled his way past the opponents for tip ins.

Heinsohn scored 17 baskets on those 33 shots. He lived up to all of the nicknames he had acquired during the season: "Tommy Gun," "Ack Ack," and "The Gunner." Such names, among basketball players, are impolite references to the fact that a man shoots too much. They are not compliments. But Heinsohn was not insulted. "What are you supposed to do with the ball, eat it?" he said in his own defense. "Let them eat it if they want to. I'll take my shots when I have 'em."

Tom Heinsohn took his first shot at a basket at age eleven. His family had moved to Union City, New Jersey, across the Hudson River from New York City. He was among the tallest boys in his sixth grade class. The schoolyards of Union City were good classrooms for a budding basketball player. The competition was keen and the kids were tough. They played to win. A youngster learned what he had to do to survive.

But the schoolyards were piled up with snow during the winter months. The bitter cold turned fingers into icicles. There were no indoor courts for 11-year-olds. There was, however, the St. Joseph's Catholic Club, where the main activity was bowling. Young boys were needed to set pins. Tommy Heinsohn became a pinboy.

The St. Joseph's Catholic Club also had an 18-by-21-foot back room with a single basket.

Tommy was allowed to use the back room whenever the alleys were empty.

That back room was a far cry from Boston Garden. The lighting was poor and the ceiling was low. A beam ran across the ceiling, forcing the players to shoot without an arc. This was the place where Tommy started to shoot "line drives," a habit he never broke.

He spent a lot of time in that back room during the next three years. He perfected his shooting and practiced dribbling and handling the ball. He learned how to use his weight and strength to advantage under the basket. By the time Heinsohn was ready to enter high school, he had developed a reputation as a basketball player around the schoolyards. The coaches and officials at St. Michael's High School in Union City had heard about him. They offered him a scholarship to attend their school and play basketball.

As a freshman, Heinsohn played on the junior varsity team. During his sophomore year, he was promoted to Coach Patrick Finnegan's varsity. The team, known as the Fighting Irish, had a losing record that season, but it would be the last losing team that Tommy Heinsohn played for.

Finnegan was a good coach for Heinsohn. The team played a running game with many give-and-go plays. Heinsohn learned to move without the ball. He learned to hustle downcourt on fast breaks and to handle the ball. He was becoming a polished ballplayer.

As a senior, Tommy Heinsohn was the star of the team. He was the 6-foot 5-inch backcourt man, an inch taller than the team's center but more agile. He made the high school All-America team, and he was picked to play for the North in a high school All-Star game in Murray, Kentucky. Many colleges were interested in him.

Heinsohn wanted to attend medical school after he was graduated from college. Most of the colleges who were after him told him that this would be no problem. But the Holy Cross College recruiters said that combining basketball with the difficult pre-medical classroom work might be too much for him to handle. "I thought," said Heinsohn, "that they were being honest with me." He enrolled at the Worcester, Massachusetts school.

The Crusaders were a basketball power in the early 1950s. Coached by Buster Sheary, they played the New York-style running game at which Heinsohn excelled. They used a five-man weave in which every man was required to handle the ball. Heinsohn fit right into the system.

Togo Palazzi, another New Jersey native, was the star of the team during Heinsohn's sophomore year. The Crusaders compiled a 26-2 record in 1953-54 and won the National Invitation Tournament in New York's Madison Square Garden, defeating Duquesne for the title. Heinsohn and Palazzi both scored 20 points in the final game.

The next season Palazzi—the Number One draft choice of the Celtics—was gone. Heinsohn, a junior, was given the task of leading the team. The Crusaders started slowly. They lost the final of the Sugar Bowl Classic on New Year's Eve to Notre Dame, 74-69, but Heinsohn was voted Most Valuable Player of the tournament. The Crusaders avenged that loss with a 95-57 victory later in the season.

Selected for the 1955 NIT, Holy Cross ran into St. Francis of Loretto, Pennsylvania, in the quarter-finals. Heinsohn outscored the talented Maurice Stokes, 28 to 21, boosting his season's average to 23.3 points a game. But little St. Francis ousted Holy Cross, 68-64. Holy Cross finished with a 19-7 record.

As a senior, Heinsohn was team captain. A new coach, Roy Leenig, wanted Tommy to play in the pivot. He responded by averaging 27.4 points, seventh in the nation, and ranking eighth among the rebounders. The team's record was 22-5 and the twenty-second victory, scored in the final game of the regular season, was a big one

A rare moment—Heinsohn versus Russell. The future Celtic teammates once competed in a college tournament in New York.

for Heinsohn. He totaled 51 points to lead Holy Cross to a 111-75 walloping of arch-rival Boston College.

The team went to the National Collegiate Athletic Association tournament that season and was eliminated by Temple in its first game, 74-72, but Heinsohn closed a great college career with 26 points. He was on everyone's All-America team.

The Celtics made Heinsohn their first choice in the 1956 draft, and Tommy decided to forgo the Olympic trials to tour with a college all-star team against the Harlem Globetrotters.

Tommy's first training camp with the Celtics was a grueling experience. He thought he reported in good physical shape, but he soon learned that "good" wasn't good enough. The two-a-day workouts under Red Auerbach were torturous. The calisthenics seemed to be endless, and the scrimmages were murder. He was a rookie being put to the test.

Often, when Tommy went up for a shot, bullish Jim Loscutoff would poke him in the midsection. Or quick Jack Nichols would reach up with one hand to play the ball and flick Heinsohn's arm with the other, destroying the accuracy of the shot. Or Bob Cousy would throw a pass over his head on a fast break—then scowl, complaining that the rookie wasn't running as fast as he could. It was quite an education.

By the time Heinsohn reported to New York to play with a rookie all-star team against the Knickerbockers in Madison Square Garden, he had a few tricks of his own. He was ready to compete with the professionals.

Heinsohn was the high scorer for the all-stars in that game with 24 points. That was when the jokes started.

"His arms will give out before his legs," someone wisecracked. "Maybe," contributed another wit, "he doesn't realize that the pro rule says *anyone* on a team must take a shot within 24 seconds, not just him."

But Auerbach was not perturbed by Heinsohn's shooting. He finally had an offensive forward who could go to the basket, a tough guy who could score points and rebound.

"Listen," said Auerbach, "when I don't want you to shoot I'll tell you." He never did.

The Celtics were not the same team at the start of the season as the one that represented Boston in the playoffs. Bill Russell, drafted by St. Louis and traded to Boston before the season opened, was playing for the United States Olympic team in Australia. So was K. C. Jones, Russell's teammate at San Francisco and the Celtics' second draft choice. Veteran Frank Ramsey was in the Army.

Arnie Risen, a skinny veteran, was the center.

Cousy and Sharman were in the backcourt. Heinsohn and Jim Loscutoff were the forwards. Palazzi and Jack Nichols were the top substitutes.

By the beginning of the season, the veterans were through testing Heinsohn. Now they were helping him. Nichols, the man whose starting job had been taken over by Heinsohn, gave him scouting reports on the opposing players. He told him to watch out for Philadelphia's Paul Arizin, who would fake a drive but seldom go to the basket. He told him to give Minneapolis' Vern Mikkelsen the outside shot and make sure that he blocked Mikkelsen's lane to the basket to stop him from getting rebounds. He warned him about Syracuse's Dolph Schayes, who had a bagful of shots under the basket.

Heinsohn was a good student. He drove and he rebounded and he snarled at referees, drawing technical fouls and fines. He developed a reputation as a tough guy. At that time Sweetwater Clifton of the Knickerbockers had the reputation of being the toughest guy in the league. Heinsohn tested him in the first game between the teams, using his sharp elbows.

"Don't ever do that again," Clifton warned.

Heinsohn studied the serious expression on

Heinsohn scored 37 points in the 1957 NBA championship game against St. Louis.

Clifton's face and answered, "Yes sir, Mr. Sweet-water." He did not pick on Clifton again. There were others.

Heinsohn blended in perfectly with the other Celtics. Cousy developed confidence in him and flipped the ball at Heinsohn without looking. Tommy was always ready. He had the knack of getting a jump on his defensive man. Cousy had anticipated the move and could hit him with a pass for a basket. The Celtics were rolling.

By the time Russell joined the team in December, Boston was leading the Eastern Division by seven games. When Ramsey was discharged by the Army in January, the Celtics were a cinch to finish first.

That same season Heinsohn was picked to play for the East in the NBA's midseason All-Star game at Boston. He did not disappoint his fans. He fired up 17 shots in 23 minutes, making five of them, and finishing with 12 points.

"You handled the ball 19 times," teased Andy Phillip, a teammate on the Celtics, "and you took 17 shots. That's not bad, considering that you were passing it in from out of bounds the other two times."

Heinsohn ended the season as the third high scorer on the team with a 16.2 average, trailing only Cousy and Sharman. He used his height and bulk to advantage under the boards, trailing only

Celebration in Boston in 1964. Heinsohn, Auerbach and Russell ended most of their seasons this way—on top.

Russell and Loscutoff among the Celtic rebounders.

Heinsohn was even more effective during the ten playoff games—three against Syracuse and seven against St. Louis—averaging 22.9 points. A player who had thrived during the first year of pressure in the rough-and-tumble jungle under the NBA backboards, he was named the Rookie of the Year.

Heinsohn played eight more seasons for the Celtics; in seven of those seasons the Celtics were world champions. When he retired at age 30 in

1965, Heinsohn had compiled an 18.6 career scoring average and had pulled down 5,749 rebounds in 654 regular-season games.

Some people thought that Heinsohn's retirement was premature. He could have played several more seasons. But he was hobbled by a ripped muscle in his left foot. He had lost that quick first step and was running into people rather than around them. He had spent too many hours trying to soak the aches out of his body in the whirlpool bath in the Celtics' dressing room. He knew it was time to quit.

"I was just another guy out there," said Heinsohn. "I had other avenues, including a real fine business offer. I didn't want to finish up sitting on the bench. To me, that means you're playing strictly for money. I wasn't. I got a kick out of playing ball. It wasn't there any more. If there's no kicks, what's the sense of suiting up?"

6

BIG BELLS

WALTER BELLAMY

by NEIL AMDUR

Walt Bellamy took the pass deep in the pivot, faked to his left, turned right and tried the jump shot. To his surprise, a big hand swiped down at the ball and batted away the shot.

Moments later, again deep in the pivot, Bellamy received another pass from a Chicago Packer teammate. This time, instead of turning for a jump shot, Bellamy decided to drive to the basket against the opposing Philadelphia Warriors. "Big Bells," as he is known, made his fake, drove around one defender and raised his long arms to dunk the ball. Again a big hand swooped seemingly out of nowhere and slapped the shot out of bounds while the crowd in Chicago Stadium roared in disbelief.

During the next three minutes, Bellamy had

the same frustrating results on two more shots. Each time, as the basket seemed to be within easy reach, the hand would defiantly repel Bellamy's bid for a basket. After the fourth blocked shot, Bellamy moved dejectedly up the court to his spot on defense. A hand reached out and patted him on the back. It was the same hand that only seconds before had shot out in front of Bellamy's face as he tried another futile jumper.

"Better luck next time," a deep voice said. The 6-foot 11-inch Bellamy turned to see the imposing figure of 7-foot 2-inch Wilt Chamberlain moving by. Chamberlain smiled, as if to say, "Welcome to the club, Walt. You're a pro now."

Big Bells' introduction to Chamberlain during the 1961-62 National Basketball Association season was one way to get acquainted with the biggest of the big men. For a rookie like Bellamy, however, it was somewhat of a shock.

Bellamy's first meeting with Bill Russell, the celebrated center of the Boston Celtics, was equally revealing to the young All-America from Indiana University who had just joined the Chicago Packers.

Russell, like other centers in the NBA, had received a scouting report based on Bellamy's early exhibition games. The report said: "Big, strong, goes to the offensive boards well." But it also said: "Favors right side almost exclusively on drives to basket."

Fortunately, Bellamy heard about the report before the night his team, the newest in the NBA, played the world champion Boston Celtics. Early in the game, after taking a pass from a Chicago teammate, Bellamy made an initial move to the right, as if he were going to drive to the basket. Russell, a cat on defense, anticipated the move and quickly moved his long, lithe body in to block Bellamy's shot. As Russell moved, Bellamy changed directions and drove in from the left side of the basket for the easiest, and certainly the most satisfying, two points of his rookie season.

As he hustled back up court in that loping, lazy stride, Bellamy smiled and shot a quick glance in the direction of the Chicago bench where Coach Jim Pollard was sitting. Pollard was grinning with his thumbs raised—the sign of success. For the remainder of the game, Bellamy played as Russell's equal and finished with 21 points, a remarkable showing for a raw newcomer against the finest defensive player in professional basketball.

Bellamy's arrival in the NBA was greeted with some of the same excitement that had followed that of Russell and Chamberlain years earlier. And with good reason.

Bellamy was a near 7-footer who packed 245

pounds. He was considered the first truly all-around big man who would challenge Russell and Chamberlain, the two giants of that era. Walt had been an All-America at Indiana, a member of the victorious United States Olympic team in 1960 and had toured briefly and successfully with a college all-star squad against the Harlem Globetrotters before signing a pro contract.

More important, Bellamy had been the subject of an intense bidding war between two leagues: the established NBA and a new pro league, headed by Abe Saperstein, founder of the Harlem Globetrotters. The NBA team had a new franchise in Chicago and wanted Bellamy, from nearby Indiana, to be its big drawing card.

Bellamy was drafted Number One by both leagues—Chicago in the NBA and Cleveland in the American League. Both groups offered him lucrative contracts. But challenged by the prospect of playing against Russell, Chamberlain and the other NBA stars, Walt signed a two-year contract with the Packers for an estimated $100,000.

"I didn't know what I was getting into," Bellamy said, "but I found out in a hurry."

Bellamy quickly discovered that playing five

Rookie Bellamy (8) was able to hold his ground against veteran Bill Russell (6).

games a week among the giants in pro basketball was considerably tougher than the two-games-a-weekend schedule he had played at Indiana.

In an early exhibition game, Bellamy learned the difference between playing for fun and playing for money. The Packers were meeting St. Louis, and one of the Hawks was shooting a foul. The shot caromed off the front rim and Bellamy moved in for the rebound. But before Walt could position himself to block out underneath, one of the Hawks had quickly stationed himself in the foul lane, gone up for the rebound and tapped the ball over Bellamy into the basket.

In another game, Bellamy had fought for rebounding position under the basket. But when he tried to jump he felt as if he were nailed to the floor. An opponent was standing on Bellamy's shoe.

The intimidation did not stop there. Against the Knickerbockers one night, Bellamy had positioned himself and was ready to make a turn-around jump shot when he suddenly realized that he could not turn. A New York player was holding onto the back of Walt's basketball pants.

During an early-season confrontation with Walter Dukes, another 7-footer in the pros, Bel-

Walt learned the tricks of the trade early in his rookie year, as demonstrated by this rebound against the Knickerbockers.

lamy and Dukes jostled hips under the basket. "We're the big boys," Dukes told Bellamy. "These are some of the things you're going to have to learn up here." Dukes moved into a defensive position, but Bellamy faked right, went to the left and scored easily. "Who's learning now?" Bellamy shouted to Dukes as they ran back up-court.

"Jim Pollard was a great asset to me," Bellamy said of his coach, who had played with George Mikan on the great Minneapolis teams. "He told me how to block off, how to broaden my base in terms of playing the pivot and what to look for when centers begin to back up."

Pollard also told everyone, including Bellamy, that the Packers were building their new team around the big man. Bellamy seemed to respond. He clicked off a string of 25-point scoring performances. By the mid-season All-Star break, there was only one choice for center on the Western Division All-Star team, and that was rookie Walter Bellamy.

Coaches were saying that Bellamy was a super-star in his first season, that he "was a combination of Russell on defense and Chamberlain on offense."

Such praise was more than Bellamy had received in high school or college. Born on July 24, 1939 in New Bern, North Carolina, a small manufacturing and fishing community 103 miles from Raleigh, Bellamy had few of the advantages that had helped make Chamberlain or Russell heroes.

For one thing, high schools in Bellamy's town were segregated. So he attended all-black Barber High School, instead of the white school where most of the star athletes played and received the recognition that got them college scholarships.

Bellamy grew up on Jones Street, a dirt road in New Bern. His father worked as an engineer for a light company and loved sports. But the big sports in New Bern, North Carolina at the time were football and baseball—not basketball. So Walter went out for end on the football team and practiced basketball when he finished the chores around the house.

"I was always tall for my age," said Bellamy, whose father stood 6-feet 5-inches tall. "But when I was fourteen or so, I shot up from 6-1 to 6-5 all of a sudden."

Bellamy was not a natural athlete in the strictest sense. Thus any skills he developed in basketball were the product of his own hard work in addition to his natural physical abilities. Bellamy skipped rope to improve his footwork and lifted weights to strengthen his arm and shoulder muscles. This may account in part for his size-46, extra-long jackets.

Bellamy's personality, unlike Russell's and

Chamberlain's, was rather quiet. To those who did not know him well, he sometimes gave the impression of being moody.

But Bellamy enjoyed modern jazz and relaxation off the court. "I need to create a little excitement from the feeling that builds up during a game," he once told a reporter at Basin Street East, a New York night spot. "I want to clap my hands to something and just enjoy myself. I like to beat the piano, beat the drums and blow a little trombone. I bet you didn't know I played the trombone in my school band." Bellamy also played basketball, and this is what won him a scholarship to Indiana.

Few large universities had heard of Bellamy in high school. Fortunately, Walt met Wally Choice, an Indiana player, while spending summers in New York and New Jersey. Choice told Bellamy about Indiana. Bellamy's high school coach, Simon Coates, also was taking summer-school courses there. When Bellamy selected a college, Indiana was the logical choice.

Bellamy's progress at Indiana was not quite as rapid as it would turn out to be during his rookie season in the NBA. As a sophomore, he averaged 17.4 points and shot 52 per cent from the field. As a junior, he averaged 22 points. His 29-point average as a senior earned him All-America honors.

In 1968 Bellamy became a Detroit Piston. Traded often, he suffered the frustrations of never having played with a winner.

As a pro, Walt continued to improve. Although the new Chicago team finished last in the NBA during Bellamy's rookie season of 1961-62, Walt reached the top. He averaged a remarkable

31.6 points per game (only Chamberlain scored better), made 51 per cent of his field-goal attempts to lead the league, and grabbed almost 19 rebounds a game (third best in the NBA behind Chamberlain and Russell). When the balloting came for Rookie of the Year, it was just a formality. Bellamy was a shoo-in.

"The big question now," said one pro coach, "is whether Bellamy is a one-year wonder or a legitimate pro star."

Bellamy answered the skeptics during the 1962-63 season. He scored 2,233 points and averaged 27.9 points per game. The following year, after the team moved to Baltimore, Bellamy again passed the 2,000-point mark (2,159), averaging 27.0 points per game. In 1964-65, he averaged 24.8. Walt was traded to the New York Knicks during the 1965-66 season and he continued as one of the NBA's most accurate shooters. In 1968-69, he was traded again, this time to the Detroit Pistons.

It was disheartening to be traded around the league. But Walt was a very good big man on the basketball court and he knew that no matter how well he played, the critics forever would be comparing him with Chamberlain and Russell. Walt accepted his fate quietly and answered his critics the best way he knew how—by continuing to play the game to the best of his ability.

7

CRYBABY GROWS UP

TERRY
DISCHINGER

by JACK ZANGER

The ball arched lazily toward the hoop. It crashed against the rim, missing the basket, then slithered off the backboard. Up for the rebound went Terry Dischinger, the 6-foot 6-inch sophomore forward of the Purdue Boilermakers. But an opposing player was leaping for the ball, too, and he slammed into Dischinger, very hard. Dischinger went down, more embarrassed than hurt. He lay there on the floor, secretly hoping the referee had spotted an infraction, but no foul was called. Disgruntled, he got up and resumed the chase downcourt for the basketball.

After the game, an assistant trainer came over to him in the locker room. "You'll never live down that crybaby reputation," he told Terry, "if you don't get rid of it as a sophomore." Terry nodded his head. He understood. He had fallen into the habit of feigning injuries and complaining to referees. But in doing so he realized he was only hurting himself.

The episode occurred during the 1959-60 basketball season. But Dischinger has never forgotten the lesson it taught him. He could see that the trainer was right, that all the free throws in the world wouldn't make up for the harm he was doing himself as a player.

Terry's mother was also helpful during this critical period. She wrote him a long philosophical letter in which she told him he "was engaged in an activity that had a lot of influence . . . that lying on the floor and complaining wasn't the thing for the youngsters who idolized him to see." The letter seemed to have good effect on him, even though he found her frank words a little hard to take.

Terry was not characteristically a whiner. On the contrary, he was an extremely serious-minded and dedicated young man who had drilled himself into becoming an all-around athlete at Garfield High School in Terre Haute, Indiana. But the more he improved the more dissatisfied he was with his performance, whether in basketball, baseball, football or track—sports in which he had earned letters. He was a perfectionist who never seemed satisfied with anything he did.

An all-around sports star, Dischinger also played baseball for Purdue.

In college, as one of three sophomore starters on the Purdue basketball team, he led a double life. On the court, he played at a furious pace in an effort to lead the Boilermakers to a Big Ten title. But in addition to being a superb athlete, he was also an honor student. He had come to Purdue on an academic scholarship rather than an athletic grant. He was studying chemical engineering. It wasn't easy to try to wedge in sleep after spending long afternoons on the basketball court and longer evenings with the books. During his sophomore year, he averaged only two to four hours of sleep a night. His nerves became frayed and his slender body began to wear thin from the bruising contact he took on the court.

With Terry as the team's leading scorer, the Boilermakers became surprise contenders in the race for the Big Ten title. A lean and graceful athlete, Dischinger tossed in long one-handers with deadeye accuracy, and despite his lack of bulk he went to the basket for layups and rebounds.

In the crucial meeting with defending champion Ohio State, Terry played against another outstanding sophomore, Jerry Lucas. They proved to be a relatively even match with Terry scoring 32 points and grabbing 10 rebounds, and Jerry scoring 27 points and taking 13 rebounds. But Ohio won, 85-71, and Purdue's dreams of the Big Ten championship vanished with the defeat. Dischinger finished the season by making some All-America lists, setting seven school scoring records and leading the Big Ten in scoring with 384 points, a feat few sophomores ever achieved. But Terry was no ordinary sophomore.

After the season, he was invited to try out for the United States Olympic team which would be competing in Rome during the summer. Again, this was a rare honor for a sophomore, especially with such great All-Americas as Oscar Robertson and Jerry West already virtually assured of places on the team. Yet Terry made the team and went to Rome that summer as the youngest cager ever to play for the U. S. Olympic five. As Olympic Coach Pete Newell said: "Terry is extremely talented and, what's even better, he makes use of this talent. I was impressed with his all-around basketball game and I was even more impressed with the wonderful way he learns. A coach loves to help a boy like that. You tell him something and he works at it for hours." Terry made quite a hit in Rome, finishing third in overall scoring behind Robertson and West.

After his return to Purdue for his two remaining seasons, Terry was a much more mature basketball player. The trip to Rome added to his confidence. Although the Boilermakers never did win that coveted Big Ten title, it was through no fault of Dischinger's. In his three varsity seasons, he set Big Ten records for most points in a season (459), most points in three seasons (1,248) and most points in one game (52). He made All-America and was among the most prized college players eligible for the pro draft.

Yet Terry wasn't certain he wanted to play professionally. He was afraid basketball might get in the way of his career. Chemical engineering, after all, was his goal. "You go to a school and you have all this technical knowledge," Terry said. "Then you get out of school and you forget it awful quick."

At first he declared that he would not play pro basketball, and in the summer of 1962 he went to work for the Phillips Petroleum Company, which had an outstanding amateur basketball team. This would give Terry a chance to play basketball if he wanted to. Despite his reluctance to play in the NBA, he was drafted by the Chicago Zephyrs. The team owner, who knew of Terry's earnestness with regard to his work, got a sudden inspiration. He contacted an acquaintance who operated a large baking concern in Chicago and persuaded the man to hire Terry as a chemical engineer during summers. Then he asked Terry to reconsider his decision.

With an arrangement like that, the young player could scarcely say no. In 1962, he was signed to a Chicago contract estimated at $20,-000, with a clause stating that he could not be cut from the team. "Chicago did offer me more money than I could make at Phillips," he explained. "But Chicago also got me the job. Without the job, all I'd have is the basketball contract."

Although Dischinger was just a rookie as far as the pros were concerned, he had a special agreement with the Zephyrs which permitted him to skip certain games if they interfered with his studies. He still had to complete some credits for his degree at Purdue and he wanted time off, as needed, to attend classes. It was agreed that he would play in all the home games but only in a limited number of the road contests during his rookie season.

In the case of most NBA rookies, team officials would have frowned upon such a plan. But the Zephyrs felt Terry was worth this special concession. He quickly proved they were right, too. Three weeks after training camp opened, he appeared for his first intra-squad game. He had been back at Purdue to attend some lectures, working out on his own in the school gym. He arrived just before the game was to start. Player-coach Bob Leonard remembers the scene clearly.

"He came in for the game and we showed him the plays 15 minutes before the game," Leonard recalled. "He really showed me something. You'd have thought he'd been working longer than we had. He learned all those plays in 15 minutes."

But when the season opened, Terry found the early going tough. He had to adjust to the pro brand of basketball. "The first couple of games, I was lost," he said. "Breaking into the league was like starting all over again. I was thrown in with the best players in the world. It was a whole different system. Centers blocked shots on you."

For a while, things looked bleak and, indeed,

someone with less dedication than Terry could have become discouraged. "I needed one game, one good game," Terry said. "I needed confidence. I scored three points one night against Boston. I was so bad it was funny. I missed the basket four times. I don't know how many times I palmed the ball."

Coach Leonard, who also played in the Zephyr backcourt, came up to Dischinger a few nights later and tried to help him find himself. "Why don't you try coming in a little closer to the basket before taking your shot?" he asked. "Try to relax more. It will come." Leonard even assured Terry that he would help set him up, get the ball to him when Terry was in good scoring position. Leonard even carried this to an extreme, actually dribbling up and handing the ball to Terry. Terry began to fire away at the basket. The ball started tumbling in. The beauty and timing and accuracy of his soft, one-handed jump shot gradually began to come back, and his scoring became more consistent. He scored 37 points against the St. Louis Hawks one night. After that, things were all right.

By midseason, he was one of the league's brightest stars; so good, in fact, that he was the only rookie named to play in the annual All-Star game. "This is no ordinary boy," Bob Leonard

Despite a late start, Terry (43) adapted quickly to the pro game.

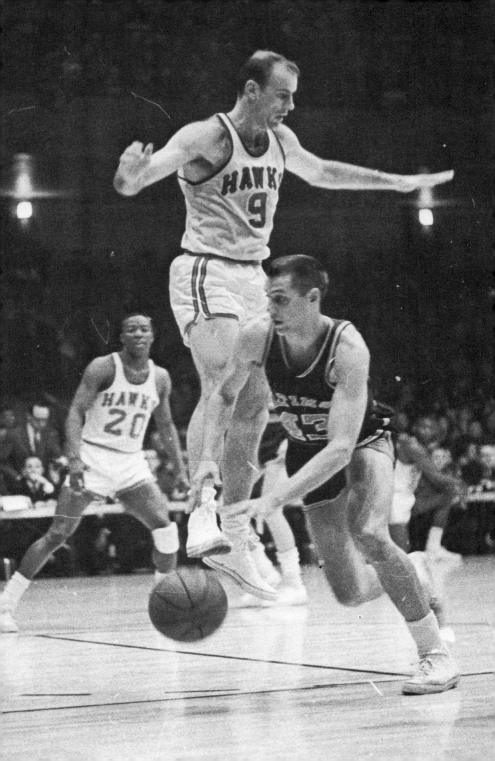

said. "He wants to play. As long as he can do the job, he'll play. He has a tremendous amount of pride in everything he does. He's a real good kid to have on the ball club. He's got a great temperament. Oh, he makes mistakes. But he strives to improve himself after every game."

Terry's progress continued as the NBA season rolled into its second half. He hit with a better than 25-point average. His jump shots were the talk of the league. And he continued to wrestle rebounds away from bigger and stronger opponents. Always, it was his insatiable desire to excel that made the difference.

At the conclusion of the season, he was named the NBA's Rookie of the Year. The record book shows he deserved the honor. Dischinger scored 1,452 points for a 25.5-point average even though he missed 23 of his team's 80 games because of his studies. He set an NBA record for field-goal percentage by a forward with 51.7 per cent marksmanship, made good on 77 per cent of his free throws and played a total of 2,304 minutes. He also took down 468 rebounds, not a bad record for a player with a slim physique.

Terry admitted he had taken quite a pounding under the boards from such tough opponents as Bailey Howell, Rudy LaRusso and Ray Scott, each of whom outweighed him by from 15 to 20 pounds. But he gave nothing away to them on the floor, often outscoring them in man-to-man duels. He was understandably elated by his rookie performance. "I knew I could make it," he said. "I always wanted to try the NBA."

Bob Leonard gave him a pro's salute. "He's on the verge of being a superstar right now," he said. "As a rebounder, he's adequate. He doesn't have the size or weight you'd like a pro forward to have. But he picks off a lot of rebounds by instinct, and his shooting moves are great. They outweigh what he lacks."

Whatever Terry lacked, he never was short of determination and drive, intangibles which manifested themselves while he was still quite young. He came from a deeply religious family, which instilled in him an abiding faith while he was growing up in Terre Haute.

"Ever since he was a small boy," his mother said, "Terry demanded perfection of himself. He couldn't tolerate any mistake. When he was in the fifth grade, his teacher said to us, 'Terry has a fault that I'd like to talk to you about. It worries me. He becomes too upset when he does something wrong. This could be a terrible thing. Every time I hand back a paper to him that isn't perfect, he cries.'"

Both Terry's parents realized the problem and worked to correct it. With their help, he learned to curb these outbursts, but not before running

up against some major setbacks. When he was in the seventh grade, he contracted a painful and serious knee ailment, and a year later doctors discovered that he had a heart murmur. They told him he would have to stop playing ball. "I thought it was the end of the world," he said.

The bitter discouragement that followed helped Terry find inner strength. His mother told him that she believed such things happened for a purpose. In this case she felt it was meant to teach him patience. People must have faith. Through the experience Terry learned patience and achieved faith in God.

A year later, the murmur was gone and Terry resumed his active sports life. He was a four-letter star at Garfield High, making all-state end in football, placing third in the state hurdles championship in track, playing first base in baseball, and making all-state in basketball. By the time he was a junior, he had received scholarship offers from more than 50 colleges.

Still, he decided he wasn't good enough in any of his sports and decided he would have to improve himself in at least one. He chose basketball and worked daily at developing and perfecting his shot. He knew he would never be big

After the Chicago franchise was moved to Baltimore, Dischinger continued to average about 20 points a game.

enough to control the boards and get by just as a rebounder, so he worked on his defensive play and improvised all sorts of training techniques that remained with him when he enrolled at Purdue. When Terry finally reached the top as the NBA's Rookie of the Year, nobody could say it had been an easy ride.

During his second year in the pros, the Chicago franchise was moved to Baltimore, where the team name was changed to the Bullets. Terry scored 1,662 points and averaged 20.8 points a game. The following season he was included in a multi-player trade which sent him to the Detroit Pistons. The Pistons slumped miserably, winning only 31 games all season, and this seemed to affect Terry's play. He scored only 1,456 points and fell to an 18.2 average. Then he entered military service for two years. When he returned to the Pistons for the 1967-68 campaign, it was clear that the long layoff had taken the edge off his shooting. In some ways, it was like starting all over again.

But Terry Dischinger had traveled the hard route before. His fans had no doubts about his being able to make his way back to the top. They knew from past experience that he had the fortitude to get there.

8

THE
ALL-AMERICAN
BOY

JERRY LUCAS

by JACK ZANGER

The sound of sneakers squeaking on the polished hardwood floor broke the silence of the near-empty gym. A practice game between the Ohio State University basketball team and the freshman squad was in progress. The yearlings were on the attack, pounding down the court on a three-on-two fast break. Cutting across from one corner came the beautifully proportioned 6-foot 7¼-inch freshman center, Jerry Lucas. He took a teammate's pass and feinted once to the right, drawing the defensive man away. Then he pumped up a one-hander that swished cleanly through the basket.

A few moments later, Lucas climbed the defensive backboard to clear a missed shot and quickly fed an overhead pass to a teammate

111

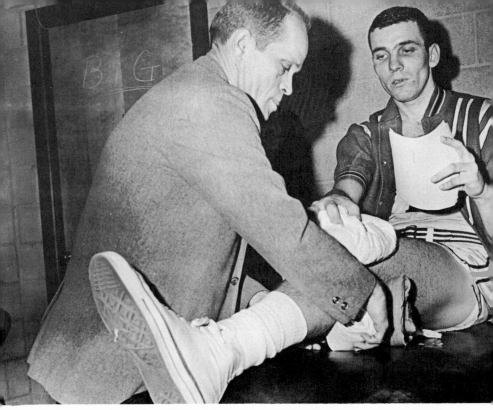

*Temporarily out of action, Ohio State star Jerry Lucas
rested while the trainer worked on a knee injury.*

downcourt. With a spurt of speed he joined the
break, took a return pass and went up for what
looked like an easy two-pointer. But in mid-flight,
he passed to another player under the basket,
who dropped the ball in for another score.

A varsity player retrieving the ball panted under his breath, "That Lucas is too much. He can
do everything." Observing from the sidelines,
Ohio State coach Fred Taylor said, "I can't wait
until he becomes a sophomore."

The pros were also waiting for Jerry Lucas.

Though he was just a college freshman, the Cincinnati Royals of the National Basketball Association had already committed themselves to making Jerry their "territorial selection" draft choice after his graduation from Ohio State. The "territorial" pick, since eliminated by the NBA, meant that a pro team could select an athlete who played within a 50-mile radius of the pro team's home base. Generally, though, the draft choice was reserved for outstanding collegians who had proved themselves in top-notch competition. Lucas was one of two schoolboys (Wilt Chamberlain was the other) whom the pros recognized solely on the basis of their high school careers.

Other fans in the country who followed college basketball during that winter of 1958 were eagerly waiting for Lucas to become a sophomore and display his skills in big-time competition. He was, after all, the most highly publicized basketball player in America. In his three years at Ohio's Middletown High, he had set schoolboy records that made him Number One on college recruiting lists. Most notable of all his accomplishments at Middletown were the 2,466 career points, (31.95 average) he scored. This broke the previous national high school record set by Wilt Chamberlain.

During Lucas' years as Middletown's greatest

athlete, the basketball team won 76 consecutive games, and captured the state championship twice. In fact, Middletown did not lose a game until the finals of the state championship in Jerry's senior year. It was the first losing game he had played in since he was a fifth-grader.

Even before he entered his senior year of high school, Jerry was the target of virtually every college recruiter in the country, especially from schools where basketball was a major sport. He was recognized as an exceptionally gifted and versatile player who could do everything on a basketball court. He could hit with precision on a variety of shots—hooks from his pivot position, one-handers from outside, jump shots from everywhere. Despite his size and his ailing knees, he could run with the fast men. As a rebounder, he had the timing to go to the rim at the right moment and the deft touch it took to tap the ball in. Best of all, Jerry was an unselfish basketball player. Sometimes his coach had to urge him to shoot more, but Jerry would shrug and say, "I get as much of a kick out of throwing a good pass as I do over making a basket. I don't particularly care about scoring so much."

But Lucas was more than a phenomenal basketball player. He was a splendid student, too. The fact that he earned A's and B's in his studies at Middletown High made him a prospective stu-

dent even for colleges with the highest academic
standards. As graduation time neared, the number of schools offering him scholarships exceeded
100. To shield Jerry from all the mounting pressure, his father established a screening program.
Mark Lucas ruled that all scholarship offers would
be reviewed first by a three-man committee con-
sisting of himself, Jerry's high school coach, Paul
Walker, and the sports editor of the Middletown
News-Journal.

In this manner, the elder Lucas felt Jerry
would be free to concentrate on his studies and
the remaining games on the schedule. Ultimately,
the choice rested between two schools: Cincinnati
and Ohio State. A month before graduation, Jerry
made his decision. It would be Ohio State. "For
one thing," Jerry explained, "it's not too far from
home, only a two-hour drive by car. My folks
can come to see me play. The main reason,
though, is that I want to get a good education.
Fred Taylor sold me. Almost every representative
who came to Middletown talked basketball first.
Fred didn't. He talked education. That's what
convinced me."

Jerry made his long-awaited debut with the
Ohio State varsity during the 1959-60 season. His
first game was against Wake Forest and Jerry
was so nervous he had to take something to settle
his stomach in the locker room before going out

Lucas (11) attempted a drive past Kentucky's Ned Jennings during the 1961 NCAA Mid-East Regional tourney.

to play. He was tight in the first half. But he unwound enough in the second half to finish the game with 16 points and 28 rebounds. Still he clearly felt he let the fans down by his showing. "I was convinced," he said, "I was going to be the greatest disappointment in the history of college basketball."

Contrary to his fears, Jerry turned out to be the rage of the college season, scoring 710 points in 27 games (for an average of 26.3 points a game), collecting 442 rebounds and leading the nations shooters by sinking 64 per cent of his shots. Moreover, Jerry led Ohio State from mediocrity to the Big Ten title and the NCAA championships, where the Buckeyes routed California, 75-55 for the title. Jerry scored the game high of 16 points against Cal and his teammates voted him their most valuable player.

Lucas was the top individual performer of the year. To no one's surprise, he qualified for the United States Olympic basketball team. Jerry played a major role in the United States victory at Rome in 1960, where he led all Olympic cagers in scoring.

His two remaining years at Ohio State were no less spectacular. As a junior, he poured 671 points into the basket for a 24.8 average, gathered 470 rebounds and again led everyone else in field-goal percentage with a 62.3 mark. In his senior year, he scored 609 points for a 21.7 average, had 499 rebounds and for the third year in a row led in field-goal accuracy with a 61.1 percentage.

Jerry's varsity years were the most successful ever in Ohio State basketball history and the period became known as the "Lucas Era." During that time, the Buckeyes rolled up 78 victories while losing only six games. They won one NCAA title and finished second in both of the other years. Jerry was an All-America selection all three years and won virtually every honor available to a college athlete. He accomplished all this while maintaining a scholastic average of 3.5 out of a possible 4.0. His final scoring figures gave him a total of 1,990 points and 1,411 rebounds. Clearly, he ranked as the greatest basketball player ever to play for Ohio State.

For four years, the Cincinnati Royals counted the days to Jerry's college graduation. Other NBA teams anxiously awaited Jerry's debut in the pros, too. Though he couldn't play for them all, he would be a great drawing card throughout the league. As an individual, as well as an athlete, Jerry would be an asset to professional basketball.

But from the very start of his college career, Lucas had said that he didn't intend to play professionally. It wasn't a question of money, Jerry maintained. It was just that he wanted to pursue a career in business. He said there wasn't enough money in the world to make him change his mind. At first, most people believed this was Jerry's way of inflating his own worth; others attributed his attitude to immaturity, claiming he would change his mind about the pros sooner or later. But Jerry stuck to his word when he got out of Ohio State. He said he had had enough of basketball.

This was depressing news for the Royals, the NBA and the professional fans who had waited so long to see him. But soon there was another

startling development. Jerry agreed to play with
a professional team called the Cleveland Pipers
of the newly formed American Basketball
League. His reasons were numerous: a contract
superior to the one offered him by Cincinnati, the
shorter schedule in the ABL, and certain other
business inducements. But Jerry never played a
game for the Pipers. The Cleveland club folded
because of financial insolvency; so did the ABL.
Jerry sat out the 1962-63 basketball campaign and
finally signed to play with the Royals the following season.

Lucas' entry into the pro ranks was accompa-
nied by as much fanfare as his collegiate debut.
Apart from coming back from a year's layoff, he
also had to make a major adjustment in his style
of play. At 6 feet 7¼ inches, he wasn't tall enough
to play center in the NBA, so he was switched to
forward. As a college center, he had done most of
his scoring with his back to the basket; now he
would have to learn to shoot while facing the
hoop. Jerry met the challenge with characteristic
determination.

"It was very difficult to adjust," Jerry would recall later. "All my life I was a center. I always had
my back to the basket. I was in close. Then
I found myself in a strange position. I was facing
the basket, farther away from it. I had to make
different moves, different shots. It took me a long

time before I felt anything near comfortable out there. I'd get the ball and the first thing I wanted to do was get rid of it. It took me a long time before I adjusted and became a basketball player again."

Jerry's first pro game was an exhibition against the St. Louis Hawks. The Hawks' star was Bob Pettit. Jack McMahon, the Cincinnati coach, advised Jerry to study Pettit's every move and try to learn from him. Pettit, too, had been a center in college, and he had also been forced to adapt himself to the forward position when he joined the pros. Now he was a super pro. Jerry had plenty of opportunity to watch Pettit that night, for the veteran played 48 minutes and practically devastated him.

"That first game against Pettit was just miserable," Jerry admitted. "Terrible. I was lost, just running around out there. They were working me over real good, picking for Pettit all night. Boy, they worked me over. Every time I turned around a guy was throwing a pick on me. From the right, from the left. And Pettit was gone. Zip."

McMahon realized from the start that he would have to be patient with Lucas. The Cincinnati coach had been around long enough to know that

With the pros, Lucas had to play a new position, which meant learning new shots and techniques.

All-America credentials did not automatically make a player—even one as good as Jerry—an All-Pro.

"It was a struggle," McMahon said. "I was real pleased with Lucas in training camp. He worked as hard or harder than anybody. He could have come in with the other attitude, you know. But his first couple of exhibition games were awful. I remember the third game we played was in Columbus, against the Knicks. The joint was packed and when Luke came out the whole place stood up and applauded for ten minutes. I've never seen anything like it. Then he proceeded to play the worst game you ever saw."

But Jerry was far from discouraged by his poor start. He refused to give up; instead, he worked even harder. When the NBA season officially opened, the Royals were matched against the Hawks and Jerry found himself once again paired with Pettit. This time Lucas scored 23 points and took down 17 rebounds as the Royals defeated the Hawks, 112-93. But Jerry wasn't out of the woods yet. "That game stood out like a sore thumb for quite a while," he said. "It was at least 25 more games before I had another good one."

But the good performances came with more frequency and Jerry began to play with greater assurance. He increased his scoring average to about 20 points a game. Even more important, he was getting the ball off the boards for the Royals, and triggering their fast break. "I realize that my big contribution to the team is rebounding," Jerry said. "When I get the ball for the team and we can get it out on our fast break, that's when we're effective."

About midway through the season, in a game between the Royals and the 76ers in Philadelphia, Jerry came up with a monumental performance as he collected 40 rebounds—a Cincinnati team record. It gave him more satisfaction than if he had scored 40 points. McMahon was as impressed as anybody else. "He has a fantastic knack," the coach said. "He gets to the ball at the peak of his jump. He teases you. You're about to get the ball and he comes and plucks it right off the top of your fingers. There are guys who jump higher than he does, but nobody has better timing."

If McMahon found any fault with Jerry, it was in the young man's reluctance to shoot more often. Jerry had deadly accuracy from almost anywhere on the floor, and the coach wanted to take full advantage of this. Gradually, Jerry began to take more shots—and connect with them. Although he still managed to come up with his nightly quota of passes to teammates who were in a better shooting position than he was, he balanced his game by shooting more himself. His all-around play did not go unnoticed; he was

Overshadowed by super-scorer Oscar Robertson, Lucas earned the respect of fellow pros for his superb rebounding and teamwork.

selected to play in the NBA All-Star game.

By the time the season ended, Jerry had amassed enviable figures for any pro, let alone a rookie. He had scored 1,400 points for an average of 17.7 a game, and his shooting percentage of .527 led all players in the NBA. Equally as impressive was the fact that in rebounds he finished behind only centers Bill Russell and Wilt Chamberlain, with 1,372 for an average of 17.4 a game. There was no way Jerry could be topped when it came time to vote for Rookie of the Year. He was virtually a unanimous selection.

Jerry's rookie year was all the more remarkable because he was playing on the same team with the man acknowledged as the best all-around player in professional basketball, Oscar Robertson. With Robertson working his magic in every game, an ordinary rookie might never have been noticed at all. But actually Robertson and Lucas complemented one another beautifully right from the outset. Jerry would haul down the vital rebound and whistle a pass downcourt to Oscar to get the fast break going. Moreover, Lucas readily accepted his role in the Royals' scheme of things.

"The offense isn't set for me," he said. "It's set for Oscar. There isn't a single set play for me except at the end of the quarter when we're going for the last shot. And then it's only just that the forward on that side gets the shot and it happens to be me."

But as good as Robertson was, there was no doubting that Jerry's presence made the Royals a better team than they had ever been before. In his rookie year, they won 55 games—the most in their history—while losing only 25. Still, Lucas had things to learn, weaknesses to overcome. "His individual defense is a fault," observed Jack Mc-

Mahon. "Around the league there's been a lot of criticism of his defense and I suppose they're right. But you can't overlook the fact that his defense suffers because he's such a great defensive rebounder. He leaves his man and goes to the board. So I try to give him a weak man to guard."

It didn't take Jerry long to learn his way around the league. He became one of the NBA's established stars during his second season. He was named to the first five on the All-NBA team and again played in the All-Star game. He has not failed to make either of these teams in the years since. As a scorer, he increased his point output to 1,414 points in his second season, and reached his career high of 1,760 points in the 1967-68 campaign. In his first six years in the NBA, he averaged just under 20 points a game and compiled a shooting percentage of almost 50 per cent.

Jerry's performance as a rebounder is even more amazing. He has finished third, fourth, third, third, second and sixth in rebounds since coming into the league. Each time he had ranked Number One among the NBA forwards.

In a poll of league coaches appraising the players, one coach described Jerry this way: "He's not a spectacular basketball player; he doesn't electrify the fans. He's what I call a 'stat' player —he gives you the same thing every night."

Which is one way of describing a pro's pro.

9

NEW
WORLDS
TO CONQUER

RICK
BARRY

by ED HERSHEY

It had not been a good game for Rick Barry. The Los Angeles Lakers had beaten the San Francisco Warriors, 135-124, and Barry, a Warrior rookie, knew he had played poorly. Now, a few hours after the game, players from the two teams walked together down a long corridor at Los Angeles International Airport. They were catching the same plane to Las Vegas, Nevada, for a rematch the following night.

While the other players talked and joked, Rick walked silently by himself.

Suddenly one of the other players caught up with Barry and began matching him stride for stride. It was Jerry West, one of the pros' greatest shooters.

"Hey, Rick," said Jerry in his soft, West Vir-

129

ginia drawl, "don't you worry about a thing. You're going to be a fine player in this league. Just don't get too concerned if one or two things go wrong. Don't get down on yourself, Rick. Relax. You're going to make it." The concern that West showed for Barry was impressive in itself, but the fact that Jerry played for the opposing team made it even more important.

Barry glanced in West's direction and smiled. "Thanks, Jerry," he said. West winked at him and drifted away, leaving the rookie to his own thoughts.

It had been a long time since Rick Barry had questioned his ability on a basketball court. As a youngster he had played basketball at a Catholic grammar school in Elizabeth, New Jersey, where his own father was the grade-school coach.

"He would take me out of a ball game if I made one error," Rick said. "I was never happy about the idea, but it worked. I'd decide, 'I'm never going to make that mistake again.' Nobody likes to be taken out of a game."

At the time, Rick was playing with and against fellows who were two or more years older than he was. But he was accustomed to the competition. Rick had started to learn the game when he was barely old enough to shoot the ball as high as the rim of the basket. As a five-year-old he would tag along with his nine-year-old brother,

Dennis, and sooner or later Dennis usually found his way to a basketball court. Even then, Rick was taller and more agile than boys his age. He probably would have excelled in any sport he tried. But basketball was the first love of his father and brother. It became Rick's favorite as well.

"My father was a strict basketball fundamentalist and a strict disciplinarian," Rick said. "He was a perfectionist. He drilled the basics into me. You know—learn how to dribble without looking at the ball, learn how to pass, learn how to run backwards."

The game was never forced on Rick. "Always, I would get interested first," he recalled. "I'd say, 'show me,' and my father would show me. Take the way I shoot fouls. He taught me to shoot them underhanded. He didn't force me to do it that way. He just said, 'I'd like you to try it this way.' I tried it and it worked."

When something did not work the first time, Barry tried it a second and a third time and, if necessary, a hundred times. He inherited more than a love of basketball from his father. He also inherited a desire for perfection.

Barry's father worked as a supervisor for the telephone company. While his two boys were growing up, the Barry family moved from Elizabeth to the more comfortable surroundings of

Barry (24) averaged 37.4 points a game during his senior year at Miami.

suburban Roselle Park, New Jersey. But plush living never seemed to affect Rick's desire to succeed on the basketball courts. He entered Roselle Catholic High School and became the star of the team. By his senior season he was also the best basketball player in the entire state of New Jersey.

Already close to his full adult height of 6 feet 7 inches, Rick was tall enough to get the shots he wanted and good enough to make them. Many colleges offered Rick athletic scholarships to play basketball for them. After considering all the opportunities available, he decided to attend the University of Miami in Coral Gables, Florida. Bruce Hale, the Miami coach, played a big part in Rick's decision. Hale, as fate would have it, was later to play a big part in Rick's life.

At Miami, Barry was sensational. He scored 2,298 points during his three varsity seasons. In his senior year he averaged a whopping 37.4 points a game to lead the nation in scoring. That same final year he became engaged to marry Bruce Hale's daughter, Pamela. With Rick listed among the best college players in the country and Pamela a beauty contest winner, they truly were an "All-America couple."

But Rick's dreams were not completely fulfilled. Practically from the day he took his first shot at a playground basket in New Jersey, Barry wanted more than anything to be a professional. And, true to his personality, he didn't want to be an *ordinary* professional basketball player. He wanted to be a star. During his senior season at Miami, Rick had heard himself described as a risky draft choice. There were respected pro scouts and officials who said they did not think

Barry would ever make the grade in the National Basketball Association. They predicted that Rick's lean, 205-pound frame could not take the constant pounding of the pro game. They also said his temper, which had flared on the court when things hadn't gone Rick's way in high school and college games, would work against him in the high-pressure world of pro basketball. They said that, as a pro, he would never get the shots he had taken as a college player.

The New York Knickerbockers had first draft choice in the spring of 1965, Barry's senior year. They decided to select Bill Bradley of Princeton, even though Bradley was committed to spending the two following years in England as a Rhodes Scholar. Rick Barry? "Too skinny," a Knick spokesman said.

Barry had grown up across the Hudson River from Manhattan and Madison Square Garden, where the Knicks played. He had seen his first pro game there. He was hurt when New York did not select him.

San Francisco had the second draft pick that year. The Warriors were not altogether certain that the Knicks' evaluation of Barry's pro prospects had been inaccurate, but Bob Feerick, the

As a rookie, Rick had to prove he could take the punishment of pro ball.

Warriors' general manager, had roomed with Miami Coach Bruce Hale while both of them were college players at Santa Clara in California. Hale, who would soon become Rick's father-in-law, assured Feerick that Barry would make it in the pros, and make it big. So San Francisco selected Barry immediately after New York took Bradley.

After the draft, Rick married Pamela, went to Hawaii on his honeymoon and then came back to San Francisco in late spring to prepare for his biggest challenge.

The Warriors' first official practice session was months away. But Barry was determined to turn himself into the kind of basketball machine that he felt he would have to become to play the grueling NBA schedule. He called old friends, haunted schoolyards and did everything he could to line up games for every night of the week. When some of the other players grew tired, Barry took off for Squaw Valley, a California resort area where Feerick and University of San Francisco athletic director, Pete Peletta, were directing a summer basketball camp.

"He'd play all day," Peletta said. "A little horseback riding, but the rest of the time he was on the court."

And when the Warriors opened their pre-season drills, the benefits of Rick's extra work were soon evident. "He reported in tremendous shape," San Francisco Coach Alex Hannum said. Hannum has a way of noting if a player is in shape the first day. He looks at his feet. Rick's feet were covered with calluses. "We hadn't been in preseason training for three days," said Hannum, "when I knew he was going to be one of my starting forwards."

Barry had proved himself before his coach and teammates. Now he had to be judged by the rest of the league. Although he played several outstanding games during the exhibition season, Rick had to show he was good enough to run, shoot and rebound with the best players in the world all season long.

At the beginning of the regular season, Rick's performances were inconsistent. He had good moments—and bad ones, too. One night, with San Francisco trailing the Boston Celtics by a point in the final seconds, Guy Rodgers, the Warriors' playmaker, stole a pass and fired the ball toward Barry, who was standing by himself near the San Francisco basket.

All Rick had to do was reach out for Rodgers' pass and make the easy layup. If he did, the Warriors would upset the Celtics. But Rick couldn't make it. The ball, which seemed to be within his reach, flew by his outstretched hands and landed out of bounds. The Warriors lost. "I felt like I was dying out there," he said in the dressing room. "I couldn't move my feet. It isn't the running in the pros that tires me. It's the way you're always struggling to break loose for a shot, a pass or a block. Guys like Dave DeBusschere and Rudy LaRusso always have their hands over me and their 230 pounds feel like 300. But I'll toughen up to them. And I'll get heavier."

Barry didn't get heavier but he did toughen up. His 205 pounds soon proved enough to conquer the grind of pro basketball. Against De- Busschere the first time, Barry had scored eight points. The second time he scored 23. Soon after, he tallied 33 against the Knickerbockers, the team that had shunned him in the draft. "He looks like he could be a real star, a superstar," Knick Coach Harry Gallatin said. By then no one in the New York organization would have called Rick Barry "skinny."

The transition from uncertain rookie to competent star was by no means an overnight occurrence. But to Barry the boost he got at the airport from Jerry West on that November night in 1965 represented the turning point.

"I was down then, and you can't imagine what it meant to me to have somebody like Jerry West,

Barry had no problem scoring against the best players in the world.

somebody I'd admired when I was in college—
even high school—come over to reassure me.
Even though we lost to the Lakers again the next
night I felt better, and I did okay after that."

Okay? Playing in all 80 games for the Warriors,
Barry scored 2,059 points for a 25.7 average,
fourth best in the National Basketball Association.
He pulled down 850 rebounds. His 86.2 free
throw percentage was second best in the whole
league. Rick was still shooting his foul shots underhanded, the way his father had suggested back
in grammar school.

Barry was named NBA Rookie of the Year on
84 of a possible 86 ballots. The other two votes
went to another standout, Philadelphia's Billy
Cunningham. In addition, Rick became only the
fifth rookie in league history to make the NBA
post-season All-Star five.

It was a year since he had become a pro and,
looking back, Rick and Pamela were happy with
the turn of events. They had an apartment over-
looking San Francisco Bay, and Rick had been
able to add some luxuries to their surroundings.
They had an expensive sports car, a handsome
English sheep dog named Rags, a stylish ward-
robe and, before Rick's second season started,
an heir—Rick Barry IV.

Still as far as basketball went, Rick Barry was
not satisfied. His temper had not caused any in-

cidents as it had in college, but it was still there. Not once, it seemed, could Barry raise his hand after being called for a personal foul without letting the official know that he disagreed. And after a missed shot, Rick's face would contort until he resembled an actor rehearsing his death scene.

"After every game, even if he scored 40 points, he would go home and think about the shot he missed and then go to practice and work on it so he wouldn't miss it again," Warrior Coach Alex Hannum said. "Heck, Rick could be the first player never to miss a shot."

Barry soon was used to the manhandling pro defenses and adjusted his game to them. His experience at Miami had given him a head start in that direction. "They used to put three men on me," he said. "It would get pretty rough near the basket. In the pros, it's one-on-one. You've just got to shove back, get their hands off you. You can't let it get you down."

In his second season Barry was the best. He scored 2,775 points, an average of 35.6 points a game, to lead the league again. He was named to the All-NBA team. Perhaps his greatest moment came in mid-season at the 1966-67 All-Star Game at San Francisco. The East, with such superstars as Chamberlain and Robertson, was supposed to win easily. Rick scored 38 points to lead

At Oakland, Barry was eventually reunited with Coach Alex Hannum.

the West to a 135-120 upset.

Barry had conquered the NBA. But again his competitive nature sent him searching for more. A new league, the American Basketball Association, installed a team across the Bay at Oakland. The Oakland Oaks offered Rick a tremendously inviting contract that included partial ownership of the team. One of the principal owners was singing star Pat Boone, who became especially convincing when he promised to guide Rick into the entertainment field. And the fact that Bruce Hale, Rick's father-in-law, was to be the Oakland coach and general manager, provided another inducement.

Rick signed with the Oaks. He sat out a season while the Warriors challenged his move in court. Then, in the fall of 1968, he began to play for Oakland. Within weeks he was leading the ABA in scoring. He also led the Oaks to first place. They had finished last the year he sat out.

"Rick is far better now than he ever was in the NBA," said Alex Hannum, who had replaced Bruce Hale as the Oaks' coach. Predictably, Rick Barry said he could do still better.

10

EARL
THE
PEARL

EARL MONROE

by BOB RUBIN

Earl Monroe made a series of lightning-quick head fakes, wiggled his body deceptively, then drove furiously for the basket. For most of the 1967-68 season, he had used these tactics to shake loose from the defensive man. But for one night the Baltimore Bullet rookie seemed to have met his match. The New York Knickerbockers' equally impressive newcomer, Walt Frazier, clung to Monroe like an octopus.

Some 18,000 fans at New York's Madison Square Garden watched with glee as Monroe drove against their man Frazier. With the ball cradled in his right hand, Monroe tried to move through the air for a right-handed layup. But Frazier, in perfect position, went up with him, prepared to stuff the ball back into Monroe's face.

It seemed so easy for a split second—then there was no ball for Frazier to stuff. While both men were hanging in the air, Monroe whipped the ball behind his back in an incredibly rapid motion and scored with a *left-handed* layup!

For a moment the crowd was too stunned to react. Then it gave Monroe an ovation. Not since backcourt star Bob Cousy of the Boston Celtics had been in his prime a decade earlier had anyone seen an exhibition of such razzle-dazzle ball-handling skill as Monroe's. And there were some critics present who dared to voice the thought that even the great Cousy might have been outshone by the rookie flash of the Bullets.

"With the things he can do, Earl Monroe makes Bob Cousy look like a little boy," declared Gene Shue, Monroe's coach at Baltimore. "That's not a knock at Cousy—it's just that Earl is a great talent. I think he's the most exciting player in basketball and maybe the most exciting athlete in all sports."

Monroe has a style all his own, a way of playing the game that makes him unique. "Monroe is funnier standing still than most men are falling down," said Coach Jack McMahon of the San Diego Rockets after seeing Earl in action for the first time. "But there's one thing no one should forget. He is also a truly great ballplayer. And he is the closest thing to another Goose Tatum I have

ever seen." Tatum, who once starred for the Harlem Globetrotters, was the greatest clown in basketball history—but also one of the greatest players.

Many of the things Earl did on the court as a
rookie certainly looked as if they had been lifted
out of the Globetrotter "play" book. He threw
blind passes to teammates, who sometimes were
as baffled by them as the other team was. He
dribbled behind his back and between his legs.
He showed a hundred different fakes and feints.
And he took—and made—some of the longest,
wildest shots ever seen in the NBA. All this, plus
his skinny pipe-cleaner legs, his gleaming white
teeth, his long upswept hair and his droopy-eyed
appearance, combined to make Earl a man who
entertained the fans all night long.

Moreover, unlike most professional athletes
who insist they ignore the sounds of the crowd,
Monroe admitted that he was well aware of the
people in the stands. "A crowd turns me on,"
he said with a grin. "I don't try to be a showman,
it's just the way I play the game. The way I play
is my style. When I do something on the floor, it's
because I think that's the way I can best get the
job done. And if it excites the fans, that's so much
to the better. I think pro basketball needs players
who can excite the fans. I don't think it can hurt
me."

Earl Monroe had been exciting fans for a long time before he got into pro competition. As a college player at Winston-Salem State College in North Carolina, his daring play earned him a nickname that carried over to his professional career. The college fans used to chant, "Earl, Earl, Earl The Pearl. Earl, Earl, best in the worl'." At Baltimore the chant was shortened to "Earl The Pearl." It could just as easily have been "Earl The Enthusiastic" based on the way Monroe approached the game. "He's just a kid who loves to play basketball," said Bullet teammate Bob Ferry. "You can tell it every time he walks onto the floor. He enjoys playing the game even more than people enjoy watching him play."

No people enjoyed watching him play more than the Bullets themselves. The year before they got Monroe, the Bullets won only 21 of 82 games. After the arrival of "The Pearl," they won 36 games. "Before Earl came, we would go into games against certain teams feeling we couldn't possibly win," pointed out Baltimore guard Kevin Loughery, Monroe's backcourt partner. "But once we got him, we began to feel that we could beat anyone on any given night. He made a great psychological difference. He's a fantastic all-around

Monroe's shots were difficult, colorful, amazing—and usually successful.

ballplayer and one of the greatest shooters ever."

Loughery's words of praise were echoed around the league, and there was little doubt, even early in the season, as to who the NBA's Rookie of the Year was going to be. It was "Earl The Pearl" by a landslide.

Monroe scored 1,991 points (an average of 24.3 per game) to rank fourth in the NBA behind three established stars—Wilt Chamberlain, Elgin Baylor and Dave Bing. Most important, instead of scoring in spurts, he scored consistently well once he got accustomed to the new surroundings and demands of pro ball. Thus the Bullets soon began to realize that they could count on Earl to deliver almost every game. No matter how rough things got, they felt they had a chance to win as long as Monroe was in the lineup.

For example, there was a brutal span at midseason when the Bullets had to play 10 games in 12 days. All of them found it tough to keep going —except Monroe. "He hardly looked like he was working out there, and he still came up with 30 points," said Loughery with a note of wonder in his voice. "You know he's got to be tired—we all were—after that stretch of games. But he went out and scored his 30 anyway."

A foul shot against New York.

Later in the season, when the rugged NBA schedule began to claim its victims, Monroe was asked to assume an even greater burden. Gus Johnson and Don Ohl, two of the Bullets' better shooters, were both out with injuries, leaving Earl practically alone to carry the shooting load. He responded by scoring 30 or more points in 11 of Baltimore's next 12 games, including a personal high and team record of 56 against the Los Angeles Lakers in February.

The Lakers won the latter game, 119-116 in overtime, but if there was ever a magnificent figure in defeat it was Monroe. He played 51 exhausting minutes. Yet when he should have been most tired, he was best. He scored 37 points in the second half, another team record. He scored the Bullets' final three points at the end of the fourth quarter to send the game into overtime. And he almost pulled it out for Baltimore in the last minute of the extra period. With the Lakers holding a seemingly safe 115-110 lead, Earl made a driving three-point play and followed it with a long jump shot to tie the game again with 1:03 to play. Though they eventually managed to win, the Lakers couldn't get over Monroe's heroics. "Unbelievable, just unbelievable," said their excitable coach, Bill van Breda Kolff.

Unbelievable is just the right word for the statistical breakdown of Monroe's performance that

night. He made 20 of 33 shots from the floor and
16 of 22 free throws for his 56 points. This was the
second highest single-game total ever scored by
an NBA rookie. (Wilt Chamberlain scored 58 in
his first year.) But when Earl was congratulated,
he shook his head. "It wasn't good enough," he
said. "We lost, didn't we?" That tells you something important about the man.

Curiously enough, Monroe had not been the
Bullets' leading prospect when it came time to
draft college players before the 1967-68 season.
As a senior in college he had averaged a remarkable 41.5 points per game to lead the country's
small-school scorers. But Earl was not well
known to the general public because few people had ever heard of the small, predominantly
Negro Winston-Salem State College. The Bullets'
preference was Jimmy Walker of Providence, the
major-college star who won Player-of-the-Year
honors.

But the Detroit Pistons also wanted Walker,
and they had first choice. So Walker became a
Piston, and, after hesitating for a moment, the
Bullets selected Monroe. They have never re-
gretted it.

What made the Bullets hesitate before choosing
Earl was the fact that Gene Shue, the Baltimore
coach, had made a special trip to North Carolina to scout him in the spring of 1967. He hap-

pened to see the only game Winston-Salem lost that year and one of the few poor games Monroe has ever played. But, luckily for the Bullets, Shue was not satisfied with one look. He made another scouting trip to see Earl, this time to the Pan-American Games tryouts in Minneapolis. There he saw the real Monroe—"Earl The Pearl." "Earl didn't make the Pan-Am team, which was a disgrace but he showed us all we had to see," Shue said.

Anyone who has watched Monroe in action in the pros would find it difficult to believe that he was once awkward and unsure of himself with a basketball. But he was. Not until he became a junior in high school did he show signs of becoming an outstanding basketball player. Soccer was his favorite sport as a young boy.

Earl's dedication to soccer helped to keep him out of trouble while he was growing up. He was born on November 21, 1944, in the slums of South Philadelphia, Pennsylvania, an area where many boys become delinquents. But Earl preferred kicking a soccer ball to joining a gang, and his mother's love and firm guidance provided further assurance that he would not get mixed up with the wrong kind of people.

"My mother was a great help," he acknowledged with pride. "She urged me to stay in school and do something with my life. And I learned a lesson from my first cousins, who lived right down the block. They got in trouble. Of course, it wasn't that easy to stay out of trouble. You had a choice of being in a gang or not being in a gang. If you chose not to, you had to avoid getting beat up."

Earl was coming home from junior high school soccer practice one fall day when he got his formal introduction to basketball. He passed a playground where some boys were playing a choose-up game and they asked him to join in. "The only reason they asked me was because they didn't have enough players," Monroe said. "I was terrible."

But though his debut was far from a smashing success, Earl was fascinated with the game. As an awkward 5-foot 11-inch tall beginner, he tried out for the junior high basketball squad and made it only because he had exceptional height for his age. The following year he went out for the high school junior varsity and was selected with the help of his best friend, a good player who pleaded with the coach to keep Earl on the squad. But even his friend couldn't help him the next year. When Earl tried out for the varsity, he was sent back to the JVs.

Players less dedicated to their sport might have quit in disgust at being cut, but Earl just worked harder. And his work proved worthwhile. By mid-season he was called back to the varsity and scored 18 points in his first start. He was on his way. As a senior at John Bartram High School, he averaged 21.7 points per game and made the Philadelphia all-city team.

The improvement in Monroe's game in one year's time amazed everybody—except those close friends who knew how many hours of practice he had put in by himself. "We'd play basketball all morning, then come home to eat about two or three o'clock in the afternoon," recalled a friend. "Then we'd see Earl heading back to the playground with a ball. We'd say, 'Hey, man, where are you going? You're not going to get any better.' But Earl would just ignore us. I have the feeling he must have known even then that he had the potential to be great."

But though his basketball skills were rapidly maturing as he neared his high school graduation, Earl still had a lot of growing up to do. For one thing, he still had to learn the value of an education. When he was graduated from high school, he decided that he was tired of school. Instead of applying for college, he took a job as a shipping clerk.

"I needed a change," he said. "I wanted to see what life was like on the outside. I wanted to see if I could enjoy it. I found that I couldn't enjoy it because I couldn't do the things I wanted to do. But I learned an awful lot while I was working. I learned what possibilities faced me without a college education and I learned that they weren't good enough for me."

Fortunately for Earl, he learned his lesson in time. After a year as a clerk, he quit and left for Winston-Salem State College.

Earl had some more growing up to do in college. First, he had to learn that basketball was second to his education. And second, he had to learn that no matter how good a player is, the coach has the final say about who plays and who doesn't.

As soon as he got to Winston-Salem, Monroe had a disagreement with Coach Clarence Gaines. Gaines felt there was no reason to break up a winning combination by inserting a freshman into the starting lineup—no matter how good the freshman was. Earl thought he should have been a starter, and with childish reasoning figured that if he couldn't start, he wouldn't stay. So he wired home for money. But his mother wisely did some checking, found out from Earl's roommate that he wanted the money for carfare home. Mrs. Monroe refused to send it. Her son was forced to stay in college.

He found it easier to change than fight. By mid-season he was a starting player, and soon he and Gaines grew as close as father and son. "I regard Coach Gaines as one of the greatest influences on my life," Earl said. "You know at some of the big schools they give the players money for expenses and things like that. Well, he didn't give me money. He gave me inspiration."

In turn, Earl gave Gaines and Winston-Salem spectacular basketball. "Whenever we needed a big basket at the end of a close game, we got the ball to our 'money shooter' and he never let us down," said Gaines.

One night in his senior year Earl scored 58 points against North Carolina College. But it was how he scored his points that really impressed people. He took 24 shots from the floor and made 22. He took 16 foul shots and made 14. In short, he was near perfect.

There were many other remarkable Monroe performances at Winston-Salem; for instance, the night he scored 68 points against Fayetteville College. However, the game that stands out in Earl's memory is Winston-Salem's visit to Akron for a regional championship meeting. "Their star was a guy called Something Smith," Earl recalled. "They had a big sign across the top of the field house, 'Earl Monroe Just a Myth, Can't Compare to Something Smith.' Well, we won the game. I scored 49. When the game was over, we had three

Alert playing by Earl Monroe helped lift the Bullets to first place during his second year in the league.

guys standing on each other to get the sign down."

But "Something Smith" wasn't anything like an Oscar Robertson or a Jerry West. As a professional, Monroe looked over the Robertsons and Wests and came to the conclusion that he wasn't in their class. In fact, he was unsure of himself on his own Baltimore Bullets team. The team already had two high-scoring veteran guards in Don Ohl and Kevin Loughery. Earl was content just to feed his teammates instead of looking for his own shots. But that ended quickly when Coach Shue took him aside one day and said, "Earl, I want you to go out and play like you did in college. You're an offensive player."

Monroe took the cue. His passing and dribbling stayed at the same quality level, and his scoring zoomed upward. So did his confidence. Ohl was traded. Monroe became the team's leader. By the end of the season, players around the league were calling Earl one of the best in the NBA. "You just pray when you're playing a guy like that," said Howie Komives, one of the better defensive men in the league. "Nothing helps. He can shoot falling down."

Earl Monroe was no one-season flash. As he gained more professional experience, his skills became even more finely polished and he became an All-Star. When the Bullets came out of the basement position and finished in first place in the tough NBA Eastern Division for 1968-69, it was Earl The Pearl who led them. He maintained his unique, crowd-pleasing style and averaged 25.8 points a game. But another great truth about Monroe became increasingly clear to the public: beneath the flashiness was a magnificent basketball player.

Official NBA Rookies of the Year

1952-53   DON MEINEKE, *Fort Wayne*

1953-54   RAY FELIX, *Baltimore*

1954-55   BOB PETTIT, *Milwaukee*

1955-56   MAURICE STOKES, *Rochester*

1956-57   TOM HEINSOHN, *Boston*

1957-58   WOODY SAULDSBERRY, *Philadelphia*

1958-59   ELGIN BAYLOR, *Minneapolis*

1959-60   WILT CHAMBERLAIN, *Philadelphia*

1960-61   OSCAR ROBERTSON, *Cincinnati*

1961-62   WALT BELLAMY, *Chicago*

1962-63   TERRY DISCHINGER, *Chicago*

1963-64   JERRY LUCAS, *Cincinnati*

1964-65   WILLIS REED, *New York*

1965-66   RICK BARRY, *San Francisco*

1966-67   DAVE BING, *Detroit*

1967-68   EARL MONROE, *Baltimore*

1968-69   WESTLEY UNSELD, *Baltimore*

INDEX

INDEX